THE NORTON SERIES ON
SOCIAL EMOTIONAL LEARNING SOLUTIONS
PATRICIA A. JENNINGS, SERIES EDITOR

Mindfulness in the Secondary Classroom: A Guide for
Teaching Adolescents
Patricia C. Broderick

SEL Every Day: Integrating Social and Emotional Learning
with Instruction in Secondary Classrooms
Meena Srinivasan

Assessing Students' Social and Emotional Learning:
A Guide to Meaningful Measurement
Clark McKown

Mindfulness in the PreK–5 Classroom:
Helping Students Stress Less and Learn More
Patricia A. Jennings

Preventing Bullying in Schools:
A Social and Emotional Learning Approach to Early Intervention
Catherine P. Bradshaw and Tracy Evian Waasdorp

NORTON BOOKS IN EDUCATION

Advance Praise

"Tish Jennings is a pioneer in bringing mindfulness into the realm of elementary school education. This book is a treasure trove of practices and tips for classroom teachers in nurturing an optimal, interconnected, and fully embodied learning environment. If implemented, the teachers stand to benefit from this approach in parallel with—and at least as much as—their students."

—**Jon Kabat-Zinn, Professor of Medicine emeritus, University of Massachusetts Medical School, author of** *Meditation Is Not What You Think: Mindfulness and Why It Is So Important*

"Dr. Jennings's book is a 'must-read' for anyone who teaches young children. By incorporating mindfulness into the classroom, teachers can create an environment that is conducive to social emotional learning and supportive of the whole child. There is absolutely no downside to teaching children to self-regulate, manage stress, and demonstrate compassion for themselves and others. It may be the most important thing they learn at school! *Mindfulness in the PreK–5 Classroom* is filled with ideas to help busy teachers make mindfulness practices a part of every school day."

—**Paige Lindblom, M.Ed., Preschool Teacher, City of Charlottesville Schools, Charlottesville, Virginia**

"I urge all readers of *Mindfulness in the PreK–5 Classroom* to incorporate the instructional scripts for guided practice and the many other gifts of this book into your classroom, school, or community setting. You will feel inspired, empowered, and amply resourced with knowledge, tools, and strategies to lead mindfulness with children."

—**Judith Nuss, SEL Consultant, Former Director of Social and Emotional Learning, Harrisburg (PA) School District**

Mindfulness in the PreK–5 Classroom

Helping Students Stress Less and Learn More

PATRICIA A. JENNINGS

W. W. Norton & Company

Independent Publishers Since 1923

New York London

Note to Readers: Models and/or techniques described in this volume are illustrative or are included for general informational purposes only; neither the publisher nor the author(s) can guarantee the efficacy or appropriateness of any particular recommendation in every circumstance.

For information about permission to reproduce selections from this book, write to Permissions, W. W. Norton & Company, Inc., 500 Fifth Avenue, New York, NY 10110

For information about special discounts for bulk purchases, please contact W. W. Norton Special Sales at specialsales@wwnorton.com or 800-233-4830

Manufacturing by Versa Press
Book design by Molly Heron
Production manager: Katelyn MacKenzie

Library of Congress Cataloging-in-Publication Data

Names: Jennings, Patricia A., author.
Title: Mindfulness in the preK-5 classroom : helping students
stress less and learn more / Patricia A. Jennings.
Description: First edition. | New York : W.W. Norton & Company, 2019. |
Series: The social and emotional learning solutions series | Series:
Norton books in education | Includes bibliographical references and index.
Identifiers: LCCN 2018057903 | ISBN 9780393713978 (pbk.)
Subjects: LCSH: Reflective teaching. | Mindfulness-based cognitive therapy. |
Stress management for children.
Classification: LCC LB1025.3 .J434 2019 | DDC 371.14/4—dc23
LC record available at https://lccn.loc.gov/2018057903

W. W. Norton & Company, Inc., 500 Fifth Avenue, New York, N.Y. 10110
www.wwnorton.com

W. W. Norton & Company Ltd., 15 Carlisle Street, London W1D 3BS

1 2 3 4 5 6 7 8 9 0

To Isaac,
You have taught me so much! I love you!

Contents

Acknowledgments

When I began my student teaching in 1979, I had the amazing opportunity to work with a gifted teacher and marriage and family counselor named Donna Schempp. She chose me as her intern because of my meditation experience and she gave me free reign to try various practices and approaches with our students. I also learned so much from her about the social and emotional dynamics of the classroom. A deep bow of gratitude to her for her patience with me and her wisdom. Years later I had the wonderful pleasure to work with another gifted teacher Alexis Harris. She has been an amazing co-author in the development of *Thrive! The Compassionate Schools Curriculum* and I have learned so much working with her.

My sincere thanks to my teachers His Holiness the Dalai Lama, Jon Kabat-Zinn, Roshi Joan Halifax, Tsoknyi Rinpoche, Matheu Ricard, Sharon Salzberg and Tara Brach. Their teaching helped me deepen my practice and give words to my experiences in the classroom.

Introduction

I began teaching children mindful awareness practices as a Montessori preschool student teacher in 1979. Having practiced myself for many years, I believed that children could engage in simple practices that would help them calm down and pay attention. In fact, I had chosen the Montessori method because I saw the potential for the learning activities themselves to become contemplative practices. I discovered that even very young children love to practice stillness, listening, and compassion.

In a sense, they are more tuned into the present moment than the adults around them. When the adults settle into a mindful and compassionate presence, children show a powerful attraction to joining this state. I found that it was relatively easy to scaffold this state for my students by modeling and "holding space" for them to engage with me. This required patience because children can't learn if they aren't given space to fail. Sitting quietly for just a few minutes is a challenge, but with time my students became accustomed to the routine of practicing at the beginning of class and during transitions. They also learned to apply the same mindful awareness to the other activities of the classroom. I was impressed at how they displayed deep powers of concentration while engaging in a simple activity, such as a puzzle, when it was demonstrated to them with slow, deliberate movements from a mindful teacher.

A few years later, I began teaching elementary school and realized that my students could lead the mindful awareness activities themselves. Each morning students took turns leading the daily practices. Mindfulness became part of the classroom culture as students realized when they needed to calm down and they suggested that we needed to take some breaths. When conflict arose between students, often one would suggest taking breaths together before they engaged in a problem-solving dialogue. In this way, my students taught me what children are capable of.

This book aims to share the lessons I learned from my years of teaching these practices to young children so you can engage your students in them and build on this experience. It is encouraging, all these years later, to see this field of mindfulness in education growing and creating mindful and compassionate classrooms around the world.

The book has three sections. In Part I, we learn about definitions of mindfulness and how it relates to social and emotional learning. In Part II, we learn a variety of mindful awareness practices that can be introduced to students. In Part III, we explore how to apply mindful awareness to creating a warm and supportive learning environment, as well as establishing routines and expectations with mindfulness and compassion.

Mindfulness in the PreK–5 Classroom

PART I

What Is Mindfulness?

Defining Mindfulness

A class of 30 preschool children sit in a circle with their eyes closed, quietly attentive. We are playing the silence game. "Let's make silence," I whisper. I give them a few seconds to settle themselves into silence. As the silence settles around us, I whisper, "When I ring the bell, listen to it ring all the way to the end of the sound and then listen to the farthest sound you can hear." As the bell rings, the children listen with rapt attention, delighted by the lush sound that reverberates through the room. Then, complete silence. After a minute or so, I invite them to open their eyes and share what they heard. Several of them describe the sound of a train: the clicking along the tracks, the sound of the whistle. Despite the fact that I didn't hear these sounds, I don't doubt that they did. Young children have much more acute hearing than adults. In fact, this is why a listening activity like this can be such a rich, engaging experience for young children.

This is an example of the many ways I led mindful awareness practices for children over my 22 years as a teacher and school leader. Between 1979 and 2001, I taught preschool through fifth grade and incorporated a variety of mindful awareness practices into my teaching. I began practicing mindfulness myself years before I became a teacher when I was 17. My practice started with Zen meditation and over the years, I have learned a variety of practices from a range of traditions, including secular mindfulness-based stress reduction (MBSR). When I decided to become a teacher, I wanted to find a way to incorporate mindfulness into my teaching. It seemed to me that if children could learn to be mindful early in their lives, it would cultivate important attributes such as calmness, clarity, and kindness that would last a lifetime. That's when I found the work of Maria Montessori and enrolled in a master of education program that included Montessori training. Before our modern era of learning and the brain, Maria Montessori understood that children have a natural inclination for creating silence, focusing attention, and engaging deeply in learning, when the conditions respect these inclinations. In today's stressful, overly distracting world, we are all yearning for silence, especially our children.

This book will provide you with the knowledge and skills you need to introduce your students to developmentally appropriate mindful awareness practices that will help them manage stress and engage in learning. First I will introduce the concept of mindfulness. I provide a brief history of the term and a secular definition that scientists use to study the effects of mindful awareness practices on our bodies, minds, and behavior. I introduce how to bring developmentally appropriate mindful awareness practices into your classroom to promote attention, engagement, and love of learning. By weaving these practices into your teaching and learning environment, you can teach children the most basic lessons in life: how to calm down and pay attention and how to be kind to one another.

What Is Mindfulness?

At its most basic level, mindfulness is awareness of what is happening in the present moment with an attitude of curiosity and openness (Kabat-Zinn, 2009). This awareness includes perceptions of the outer world that we take in through our five senses of sight, hearing, taste, smell, and touch. It also includes awareness of our inner world, including thoughts, sensations, and emotions. Curiosity and openness involve a sense of letting things be as they are, rather than grasping or rejecting them. Even if something is uncomfortable, we can be aware of the discomfort and lovingly accept it, rather than trying to push it away by distracting ourselves or ignoring it. In a mindful state, we become truly aware of the fullness of life, in all its multifaceted richness.

Mindfulness is a state, a trait, and a practice. I am in a mindful state when I am fully aware of what is happening in the present moment and accepting it, rather than trying to grasp or reject it. In a mindful state, I realize that I am not my thoughts—they are simply activity of the mind, like gurgling can be an activity of my stomach. When I am mindful, my mind is settled but not entirely quiet. Thoughts come and go, but I do not latch on to them. They are like background noise. I know they are not me; I am not my thoughts. I can easily find myself becoming attached to a thought, and it carries me into the rabbit hole of thinking—planning (or worrying about) an activity in the future, ruminating about something that happened in the past. But I can catch myself and let it go, bringing my mind back to now.

Children regularly spend time in states of rapt attention, but it is different than our experience of mindfulness because their minds have not yet developed the cognitive complexity and meta-awareness that adults have. As a child, I remember sitting in the backyard in a patch of lily of the valley, savoring the scent of the lovely flowers, listening to the birds, and watching the ant convoys trundle through the grass. I recall feeling enraptured, calm, and blissful.

In his classic book *Magical Child*, Joseph Chilton Pearce (1977) argues that the pressures of our modern world attempt to push children's developmental processes and interfere with the natural cultivation and development of contemplative states. While he wrote this book in 1977, these words contain a level of urgency that is even more relevant today. For most of human history, parents knew how to prepare their children for adulthood because life was simple and options were limited. The future was also fairly predictable. Today children and parents face a completely unknown future. If you think back just a decade, could you have predicted our lives today? Just consider how much the smartphone has changed our lives. In a world where change is so rapid, it's easy to feel anxious and worried about our children's future (not to mention our own). However, our children are observing and absorbing our insecurity, and it's causing distress in the form of increasing mental health and behavioral problems (Collishaw, 2014). The best thing we can do to support them is to develop our own mindful awareness so we are more able to manage our own anxiety and uncertainty and provide a psychologically secure base for our children to grow from. So, a key message here is that to teach mindfulness to children, you must embody mindfulness yourself. From my years of experience doing this work with preschool and elementary children, I believe that it was my own mindful awareness that scaffolded their experience of the practices.

While there is very little understanding of why, some people are naturally more mindful than others, so in this way, mindfulness is a trait or a disposition. It is also a practice. We can intentionally practice being mindful in a variety of ways, both formal and informal. With time and practice, we can become more mindful, during practice and during our everyday activities, including our time with children. Sitting meditation is a formal way to practice. But we can also bring mindful awareness into any activity or interaction throughout the day. Washing dishes can become a mindfulness practice. As I wash, I bring my awareness to the sensation of the soap on my hands, its scent filling the air around me, then mingling with the aroma of leftover food, the slick feeling of the wet, soapy dishes, the sound and warmth of the water. You can practice mindfulness in nature, sitting outside, listening to the sound of the birds and the wind through the trees. Watching a spectacular sunset, witnessing the brilliant colors through the clouds shift and fade.

As a Montessori teacher, each lesson I presented to my students became a mindful awareness practice, almost like a Japanese art, such as ikebana (flower arranging) or *chanoyu* (the tea ceremony). The lessons have a ritual quality that captures children's attention. Take, for example, a simple activity such as completing a preschool puzzle. If I introduce the new puzzle with a quality of awe and respect, young children automatically recognize that this is something important and pay attention. Sometimes I might hide the puzzle under an interesting cloth to create some added suspense. Gathering a small group of interested students sitting around a small rug, I smile at each of them with a twinkle in my eye that sends the message, "I have something fascinating to show you!" Silently with wide eyes, I lift the cloth and hold up the puzzle, so they can see it. Then I lay it down on the rug and begin to take out each piece, one at a time, holding each piece carefully by the knob with my thumb and index finger and laying each piece on the rug in the same order they were in the frame. Then I say, "I took all the pieces out of the puzzle." Next I slowly and methodically begin to return each piece to the frame in the same order I took them out, show-ing them how to turn the pieces a little to find the right fit. Once all the pieces are in the frame, I say, "I put all the pieces back in the puzzle." Then I carry the puzzle back to its place on the shelf. At this point, I might invite one of the students to complete the puzzle. I was always amazed at how well they would imitate my mindful approach to completing the puzzle. We now know more about how mirror neurons in the brain support this process of learning. In this sense, the puzzle becomes a mindful awareness practice and children learn not only to focus their attention but also to build visual-perceptual, small motor, and coordination skills. In a later lesson I would add more language, introducing the puzzle's vocabulary (e.g., differ-ent kinds of animals, trucks).

The History of Mindfulness

The practice of mindfulness has an ancient history. Different forms of mindful awareness practices (also called contemplative practices) can be found in all spiritual and religious traditions. These practices can involve formal meditation focused on prayer, song, a sound or word, a visual image, or movement, such as walking through a labyrinth or engaging in a ritual (Williams & Kabat-Zinn, 2011). Over the course of the past several decades, a secular understanding of mindfulness has emerged, primarily as a result of scientific research that has clarified both the dimensions of practice and the effects of these practices on our minds and bodies (Kabat-Zinn, 2003). The research has demonstrated that secular mindful awareness practices build basic strengths that underlie resilience and well-being, such as emotion regulation, cognitive functions, and greater attunement with oneself and others (Khoury, Sharma, Rush, & Fournier, 2015).

Mindful awareness can be directed at both external and internal experience. An excellent metaphor for this understanding was presented by Dan Siegel, a psychiatrist who developed the field of interpersonal neurobiology. He calls it the Wheel of Awareness (Siegel, 2009). Imagine your awareness is like a wheel. The hub of the wheel is the source of your awareness, and the rim of the wheel represents the world of experience that can be accessed through eight senses (see Figure 1).

Going around the Wheel of Awareness, let's start with the five physical senses. We can bring mindful awareness to our experience of the outer world

The Wheel of Awareness

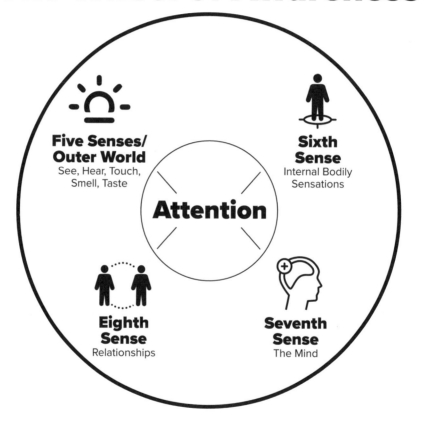

Adapted from Siegel, 2009

through our senses of sight, hearing, touch, taste, and smell. Sometimes it helps to understand mindfulness by considering mindlessness. There have been many times when, in a rush, I have eaten a snack or a meal completely mindlessly (e.g., where did that bag of potato chips go?). My mind was on other things. I was distracted by a potential conflict with a colleague or partner, or worried about finances or a troublesome physical symptom. In contrast, when I bring the fullness of mindful awareness to my experience of the world through my senses, the world comes alive. I may take one bite of a potato chip and notice how terribly salty it is and then decide not to eat it at all. I may opt to eat a piece of fruit instead and then notice the richness of color, scent, and flavor of a ripe peach or a tangerine. Each bite brings a new adventure as a panoply of tastes burst forth, tart, tangy, and sweet, with subtle tones of rich earthiness. When the senses come alive with mindful awareness, experience becomes richly textured with all the senses, simultaneously. I can focus my attention on the sounds of summer in my backyard: the cicadas, the variety of bird songs, dogs barking in the distance. I can notice how different outdoor sounds are in the winter when the leaves no longer buffer the sound of cars and trucks speeding down a freeway, a mile away. Mindful listening to live music transforms the experience. I can close my eyes and notice how the over-tones of the bass and the trombone blend to create a powerfully textured blast that reverberates throughout my entire body. I can mindfully attend to the world through my eyes, noticing the subtle detail of the bark on a tree trunk or the refined beauty of light depicted in a Rembrandt painting in a museum.

Maria Montessori recognized that children have an intense drive to refine their sensory experience. So much of the world is new to them, and their primary explorational tools are their senses. Because of this, for young children, mindfulness begins here; mindfully exploring the world through their senses comes perfectly naturally. Our role as guides is to facilitate, point out, and to name. At the beginning, it's best not to use too many words in our teaching. Let the children sense for themselves and listen to how they describe the world.

Getting back to the Wheel of Awareness, the next place on the rim is the sixth sense, which is inner bodily sensations. When we say that we have a gut feeling, we are talking about this sense. When I bring mindful awareness to my experience with this sense, I immediately notice tension I'm holding in my body. Usually it's tension in my neck and shoulders or in my jaw. I can also notice sensations in my body that let me know the stress response is being triggered. I can feel my blood pressure rise and my body warm as my body prepares me to fight or run. This sense also gives me the ability to notice sensations associated with hunger and thirst, balance, and where my body is in space. This sense helps us notice what we need, which can help us take better care of ourselves. Young children can also engage in mindfully attending to inner bodily sensations. With direction, they can learn to identify the feelings associated with emotions, stress, balance, hunger, thirst, and satiety.

Despite Western philosophy's dominant Cartesian view, mind and body are not separate. The nervous system inhabits the body from head to toe. In fact, the solar plexus, located in the center of the abdomen above the diaphragm, is a network of neurons, often called the gut's brain, because it operates in a very similar way. Its circuitry allows it to function independently. It can even learn and remember. Although it plays an important role in our sense of well-being, few people are even aware of it. Dr. Michael Gershon, a professor of anatomy and cell biology at New York–Presbyterian/Columbia Medical Center, has studied this brain for decades (Hadhazy, 2010). When other doctors diagnosed some illnesses like chronic abdominal pain as imaginary or emotional and referred patients to a psychiatrist, what they were missing was that the problem was not in their head, but in their gut. Most of the chemical messengers found in the brain can also be found in the gut brain, especially those associated with our well-being, such as neurotransmitters like serotonin, dopamine, glutamate, norepinephrine, and enkephalins, one class of the body's natural opiates. The gut brain also delivers benzodiazepines, a group of chemicals that can also be found in popular antidepressants.

In this sense, the gut has a mind of its own. Tuning into this mind can often surprise us, because in the West, we have held this idea that we live in our heads and that we are our thoughts. So when we tune into the body by bringing awareness to it, we can experience feelings that we never paid attention to before. The two brain systems (head and gut) are connected by the vagus nerves, a pair of the largest nerves in the body. The vagus nerves play a critical role in the stress response, and it is believed that mindful awareness and compassion practices can support emotion regulation by strengthening vagal tone (Vago & David, 2012).

The seventh sense is our awareness of mental activity. It is not thinking; it is awareness of the activity of the mind that we call thought. This understanding can be confusing because, as I mentioned above, we often believe that we are our thoughts. However, when we practice mindfulness, we begin to notice that our thoughts have patterns. Our thinking tends to be habitual. Once we recognize this, we can create some sense of space between our being and our thinking. It's not as if the thoughts go away. They still come and go; we're just not engaging with them. During practice, we may find ourselves engaged in a thought that has caught our attention, such as, "Oh no, I forgot to pay that bill." A thought like this can easily turn into rumination: "Why did I let that happen? What's wrong with me? Can I afford the late fee? Maybe I can get out of paying it this time." I call this a rabbit hole, because it can twist and turn into branches of thoughts that can take us into unexpected thought places. Siegel (2009) has named the ability to recognize and observe this process "mindsight." It's also the understanding that others have minds like ours, which forms the basis for empathy and compassion. We are still learning about the development of cognition in children. But it is clear that the executive functions of the brain take time to develop, and simple mindful awareness practices may be effective means for promoting these functions (Davidson et al., 2012). That said, adult meditation practices that build this capacity are likely not developmentally appropriate for young children because they don't yet have the metacognitive functions to engage in them.

The eight sense is called the relational sense, because it allows us to tune in to others. Most people have experienced walking into a room and immediately knowing that there has just been some kind of altercation. We can feel this prickly vibe that makes us hesitate a bit. What just happened here? People are angry or sad, but we're not sure why. This is the relational sense in action. While we still have lots to learn about this sense, mirror neurons likely play a role. In numerous experiments with animal and human subjects, scientists have found that neurons in our brains fire when we observe another person performing some activity. For example, in one study, scientists asked research subjects to wiggle a finger while another subject watched. In both cases, the part of the brain, the motor cortex, involved in finger wiggling fired, even though the nonwiggler was not moving his finger (Fadiga, Fogassi, Pavesi, & Rizzolatti, 1995). Mirror neurons likely help us cultivate a sense of attunement with one another (Chartrand & Lakin, 2013). Applying mindfulness to this natural inclination can help us understand others better and fit into social situations more successfully.

While explicitly practicing mindful awareness by engaging the eighth sense is quite abstract for young children, they are especially attuned to others in their life, especially their caregivers and teachers. One way to bring more awareness to this sense is to acknowledge when you are feeling it. For example, when enjoying a fun activity with children, note how good it feels to be happy together. When children and adults explicitly pay attention to the positive emotions that come with enjoying life together, it builds resilience (Cohn, Fredrickson, Brown, Mikels, & Conway, 2009).

The Wheel of Awareness gives us a template for thinking about how to apply mindfulness to our experience and to integrate mindful awareness into our teaching. Each lesson provides an opportunity to consider which sense is involved and how to employ mindful awareness to enhance learning. This is especially relevant to social and emotional learning, which we explore in Chapter 2.

A Developmental Approach

While mindfulness in education is now all the rage, some programs have been developed without consideration of children's developmental needs and the science of learning. Indeed, there is very little research to inform what practices are appropriate for children at any particular age. We must apply what we know about child development and learning science to make educated guesses about what to teach. However, it is clear that young children should not be asked to practice the formal sitting meditation that adults typically engage in for more than a few minutes. It's also unclear whether or not this is the best approach to teaching mindfulness to young children. I am concerned that if we ask children to engage in practices intended for adults, they will grow to dislike the practices.

The activities presented in this book have been time tested in that I have taught them to children over the course of my 22 years as a teacher. I know that young children can successfully engage in these activities, and I know that they cultivate mindful awareness when it is presented to children by an adult who embodies and can scaffold mindfulness. A great deal of research is still required to clarify these issues, and I want to be clear about the limitations of our knowledge regarding the effects of mindfulness on children's well-being and learning.

Two Simple Mindful Awareness Practices for Adult Beginners

Breath Awareness Practice

This practice is a basic focused attention mindful awareness practice that is typically introduced to beginners by mindfulness teachers. This involves focusing attention on the sensations of the breath and sustaining this attention. It is perfectly normal for the mind to wander off into thoughts or to become distracted by other sensations. The practice is simply to notice that the attention is no longer focused on the sensations of the breath and to return the attention to the breath. During a practice session, you may repeat this sequence—focusing on the breath, finding your mind wandering, bringing the attention back to the breath—again and again. This is the practice, so don't worry that you aren't doing it correctly. With time and practice, the mind begins to quiet and stabilize. The thoughts and other distractions become like background noise. I am aware of the thoughts, but I'm not consumed by them. It's almost like I'm hearing them from far away and I can't even really make out their meaning—a kind of mumbling of the mind, so to speak. During the practice, we also aim to cultivate an attitude of acceptance and curiosity. This is a kind and gentle openness to the experience of the present moment without judgment. To be clear, this doesn't mean that I might not notice my judgmental thoughts—I do. But I just notice them and let them go, so I don't judge my judgments. I'm not grasping or rejecting my experience but simply letting myself be with it.

After getting used to the practice and doing it regularly, people find that they are able to consciously bring this state of mindfulness into daily life throughout the day.

To begin, find a quiet place to sit where you will have no distractions for a few minutes. Sit with an upright posture on a chair or a cushion. Be sure that your back is straight, but not stiff or rigid. I like to imagine that there's a string pulling me up from the top of my head, lifting my torso. Place your hands folded on your lap. Close your eyes or lower your gaze toward the floor; either one is fine. You may wish to start with eyes closed and then experiment with open eyes later, once you have become familiar with the practice. Notice the weight of your body sitting on the chair or the cushion. Feel the substantial quality of your body, here and now, in this present moment. Now shift your attention to the sensations of your breathing. You may notice the sensation of the air as it enters and leaves your nostrils. It may feel cooler on the inhale and warmer and moister on the exhale, after the air has been warmed and humidified in your lungs. There are very small hairs on the insides of your nostrils that sense this inflow and outflow. See if you can refine your focus on this sensation.

If you find yourself lost in thought, gently remind yourself to return your attention to the sensations of the breath. Be kind to yourself, as if you were training a very young puppy to sit and stay. Like the puppy, our minds need to be reminded again and again, very gently. With time and practice, both the puppy and our minds will learn to settle.

As you practice focusing your attention on the sensations of the breath, you can also try to focus on your lower abdomen, where your diaphragm is located. This is a large, dome-shaped muscle that expands and contracts with each breath. As you focus on the diaphragm, you can feel your abdomen rise and fall with the breath. A third way to focus attention is to notice the entire pathway that the air travels in and out of your body, feeling the air as it enters your nostrils and fills your windpipe. Feel the air filling your lungs as your diaphragm rises, and then the reverse pathway as the air leaves your body. Sometimes this is experienced like the ocean, as waves going in and out.

Each time you find yourself distracted by thoughts or sensations, simply and kindly notice how your attention has shifted and return your attention to the breath. Please note that it's not expected that you will be able to completely stop your thoughts. After more than 40 years of practice, my mind still has thoughts on and off during my practice. The difference is that I know I am not my thoughts, and I experience them as simple phenomena of my mind, rather than making them the center of attention and becoming consumed by them.

If you are new to this practice, I recommend starting with 5 or 10 minutes of practice. Eventually, you can extend the time to 15–30 minutes, if you have time in your day. Doing this practice regularly can yield significant benefits. I find that my regular practice helps me start my day with a calm and enlivened mental state. The more I consistently engage in formal practice, the more I am able to practice informally, consciously bringing mindful awareness to everything I do.

Some people enjoy using one of the many apps that are now available, or downloading audio recordings of guided practices. Feel free to look for these in the appendix, where resources are listed. Listening to a guided practice can be quite helpful if you are new to this. One of my college students recently shared that he uses his Alexa every morning to remind him to practice, and it automatically starts the app for him. Experiment with the time of day, the way of sitting, and the type of guidance until you find a routine that works best for you.

Body Scan Practice

The body scan practice is another basic mindful awareness practice. The intention of this practice is to bring mindful awareness to every part of your body sequentially. Many people enjoy doing this practice lying down, but you can also do it in the same seated posture as the breath awareness practice. During this practice, we bring mindful awareness to the sensations throughout our body, similarly to attending to the sensations of the breath in breath awareness. Guided audio is readily available on various apps and on the web (see the appendix). You can begin the body scan by focusing on your head or your feet. I often begin teaching the practice starting with the head, since many people report a great deal of tension in their upper bodies and feel the need to attend to this first. However, you may find guided practices that start elsewhere in the body, and it is perfectly fine to use them.

Begin by noticing the weight of your body lying on the floor or sitting on the chair or the cushion. Feel the heaviness—the substantial quality of your body. Next draw your attention to the top of your head. Notice any sensations there. You might feel the hair on your head or tension in your scalp. Just notice, bringing mindful, open-hearted attention to this part of your body. Next bring your attention down your forehead. Do you notice any tension there? Just notice in a gentle way; don't try to resist or change how you feel. We're just bringing awareness to the body. Scan down the face to the eyebrows and eyes. See if you notice any tension or other sensations in the many little muscles in this area. Now bring your attention down your nose and cheeks. Is there any tension in the muscles along the sides of your nose and face? Bring your awareness to your jaw and chin. Are you holding any tension there? This is a place where we often hold onto stress and emotions. Just notice with gentleness and kindness.

Next bring your awareness back up to the top of your head and then down the back of your head. You may notice the weight of your head pressing against the floor or whatever you are lying on. Just notice the feeling of pressure. You may also feel your hair as you bring your awareness down toward your neck. Bring your mindful awareness to the base of your neck, where your neck and shoulders meet. This is another place where we often hold tension. Just notice what you feel with kindness.

Bring your awareness down your left shoulder, noticing any tension, perhaps feeling the weight of your body pressing against the floor here. Bring your awareness to the place where your shoulder and upper arm meet and notice how that place feels. If you're sitting upright, notice the feeling of the arm hanging from the shoulder. Is there any tension? Bring your attention down your left upper arm to your elbow, forearm, wrist, hand, and fingers. Notice if there is any tension or other sensations, such as the feeling of the clothing on your body, or the weight of your body pressing against the floor. Take a moment to see if you can focus your attention on your entire left arm and hand. Now compare your left arm and hand to your right arm and hand. Do they feel different? If so, how?

Next bring your awareness back up to the point at the base of your neck and then draw your attention to your right shoulder, noticing any tension or other sensations with kindness and openness. Bring your attention to the place where your right shoulder and upper arm connect and see if there's any tension there. Scan down your right upper arm to your elbow, forearm, wrist, hand, and fingers. Notice any tension or other sensations. See if you can feel your entire right arm and hand. Then compare your right and left arms and hands again to see if you notice anything. How do they feel now?

Now bring your awareness back to the base of your neck and slowly scan your back, vertebra by vertebra, noticing any tension in your back. Feel the muscles along your spine, the pressure of your back ribs against the floor or the back of the chair, noticing any sensations with kindness. Bringing your attention to the base of your spine, shift your attention to your left buttock and pelvis. Notice the weight of your body against the seat of the chair or the floor, and notice any tension where your pelvis connects to your left thigh. See if you can feel this joint, which is the largest in your body, connecting your pelvis to your femur. Bring your awareness down your left thigh, knee, calf, ankle, foot, and toes, noticing any tension or other sensations. See if you can feel your entire left leg and foot and then compare it to your right leg and foot. Do they feel different? If so, how?

Next bring your attention back up to the base of your spine and shift your awareness to the right buttock and pelvis, noticing any tension in the hip joint. Bring your awareness down your right thigh, knee, calf, ankle, foot, and toes. Again, see if you can feel your entire right leg and foot and compare it to the left one. Do they feel any different now?

Now bring your awareness back up to the point at the base of your neck and scan around to the front of your neck. Notice any tension here, in the front of your neck, down your chest to your clavicle and sternum. Scan down your chest, noticing any tension between your ribs or any sensations in your belly. Notice the rise and fall of your abdomen with each breath. Allow your awareness to settle in a place in the center of your lower abdomen. This is the center of gravity of your body, and focusing on this point can help you feel calm, centered, and grounded. Feel this point rise and fall with each breath, like you are floating on gentle waves in a warm salty sea. As time allows, let yourself enjoy the peaceful feeling of the gentle rising and falling with each breath. You can end the practice whenever you are ready.

Mindfulness and Social
and Emotional Learning

What is social and emotional learning (SEL) and how does mindfulness support it? This relationship is important to consider when
designing mindful awareness practices for preK–5 settings. The Collabora-
tive for Social and Emotional Learning (CASEL) has identified five primary
social-emotional competencies (SEC): self-awareness, self-management,
social awareness, relationship skills, and decision making. The first two
(self-awareness and self-management) are intrapersonal skills. These are
skills that help us understand and manage our feelings and behavior. Social
awareness and relationship skills are interpersonal skills: they help us
understand others, build healthy relationships with others, and contribute
to our community. Responsible decision making is the culmination of these
four competencies. When I understand myself and others, I am more able

to make decisions and behave in ways that take into account the needs of all involved.

Mindful awareness can be thought of as a foundational skill or building block that underlies SEC (Lawlor, 2016). Mindfulness can support SEL in two primary ways. First, when I practice mindfulness, I build my own SEC; I am more able to mindfully monitor my behavior in the moment, so I can intentionally model the social and emotional competencies I want to teach to my students (Jennings, 2015a). Since children learn these skills primarily from observing the adults in their lives, this is crucial to effective SEL program implementation (Jennings & Frank, 2015). Second, I can teach mindful awareness and compassion practices to my students as a way to augment or support their SEL. Next we examine each of the CASEL competencies and how mindfulness supports their development.

Know Thy Self

Mindfulness facilitates self-exploration and self-attunement. Simple mindful awareness practices cultivate a stillness that helps us become more aware of our thoughts, emotions, bodily sensations, motivations, and values. People who are more mindful are better at identifying and describing their emotions (Dekeyser, Raes, Leijssen, Leysen, & Dewulf, 2008). They are more attuned to their fundamental needs (Brown & Ryan, 2003). Mindful people are more intrinsically (versus extrinsically) motivated and less materialistic (Brown, Kasser, Ryan, Alex Linley, & Orzech, 2009; Brown & Ryan, 2003).

Without the intrapersonal skills of self-knowledge and self-regulation, it is difficult to understand others. These skills are also intimately related. In this way, these skills form the basis for SEL.

Mindfulness provides support for both of these skills. When I bring mindful awareness to my inner and outer experience, I can deeply know myself. I recognize the inner bodily sensations of an emotion before it erupts out of control. Based upon an understanding of my history and thinking patterns, I know why I am feeling the way I do and how these feelings can distort my perceptions and impact my behavior. I can see the situation with more clarity, openness, and curiosity, rather than from the limited perception that my emotion or stress triggers. I can see that this is happening, and I can move beyond it to recognize the needs and perspectives of others and the entire social context of the situation. Finally, mindful awareness helps me recognize and honor my physical, mental, emotional, social, and spiritual needs and helps me establish and maintain healthy boundaries between myself and others, without withdrawing or creating unnecessary barriers.

Manage Thy Self

Depending upon their age, children's sense of self and ability to self-manage is still developing. Young children are just beginning to learn self-management, which is the ability to regulate strong emotions and the impulse to behave in less than prosocial ways. The ability to self-regulate depends upon the development of the executive functions (EFs) of the brain. These functions help us plan our behavior to achieve our goals. This often requires inhibiting strong impulses. Other EFs include working memory, cognitive flexibility, reasoning, planning, and problem solving (Diamond & Lee, 2011). Executive functions are foundational for school readiness (Blair & Razza, 2007), physical and psychological well-being (Moffitt et al., 2011), and academic learning (Witt, 2011). These functions take time to develop and require opportunities to practice. Mindful awareness practices build attentional control and exercise EFs (Zelazo & Lyons, 2012) for better emotion regulation (Teper, Segal, & Inzlicht, 2013). Each time we practice focusing attention during a mindful awareness practice such as the breath awareness practice we learned in Chapter 1, we find that our attention will drift away from its target, in this case the breath. Once we notice this, we intentionally return our attention to the target, repeating this process again and again. Over time we cultivate attentional focus, inhibition, and cognitive flexibility. We also cultivate an attitude of openness and acceptance toward ourselves. These skills help us become more aware of sensations and thoughts associated with emotions and to accept them so when a strong emotion arises, we are more consciously aware of what is happening and have more mastery over ourselves. We can respond rather than react automatically from an emotional blind spot.

For example, when I'm teaching I hate to be interrupted by a student. I've got my lesson plan in my head and when a student interrupts me, it's like the whole lesson goes off-line. I forget where I was, what I was saying, and what comes next. It's especially difficult when I'm feeling time pressure (e.g., it's five minutes before the bell rings). Since I understand this about myself and the nature of my emotions, I know that I will tend to lose patience with a student under these conditions. I notice that I tend to imagine that the interrupting student is doing it intentionally to irritate me. I also know that the anger I am feeling actually promotes and reinforces this perception. So when it occurs, I can give myself some space to accept the thoughts and feelings, calm down, and question their veracity, rather than reacting automatically with an angry comment that will not only interfere with my relationships with my students, but will also inhibit the learning I'm trying to promote. I catch myself, take a breath, and notice what's actually happening. There have been times when I've been surprised by the reality of the situation—like the time a student was trying to alert me that the classroom pet rat was about to escape.

Know the Social Scene

Social awareness involves taking the perspectives of others, feeling and expressing empathy, recognizing the value of diversity, and understanding social norms of behavior. Research has shown that mindfulness and social understanding are positively related (Dekeyser et al., 2008). Furthermore, perspective taking and empathy are important elements of social awareness that have been identified as suggested outcome variables for the emerging research on mindfulness-based programs for children (Davidson et al., 2012). Compassion-based practices that involve generating feelings of care for others and oneself can also support social awareness.

Know How to Build Relationships

Relationship skills involve the ability to form and maintain positive relationships with others and to work cooperatively and resolve conflicts peacefully. These skills require listening to others. Without carefully listening, we cannot understand others' perspectives and engage in considerate dialogue, critical to relationship building and conflict resolution. However, listening is a skill that is rarely taught or practiced. The practice of mindful listening can help both children and adults build the capacity to listen more deeply to one another.

> Listening is the oldest and perhaps the most powerful tool of healing. It is often through the quality of our listening and not the wisdom of our words that we are able to effect the most profound changes in the people around us. When we listen, we offer with our attention an opportunity for wholeness. Our listening creates sanctuary for the homeless parts within the other person. (Remen, 2006, p. 219)

Listening is just one way mindfulness can support relationships skills. As I develop my ability to tune into the relational sense, I am more likely to notice subtle signals that my partner is becoming anxious or annoyed about something. I can hear the quiver in the voice of a child who is about to cry, and I can more easily imagine how another is feeling. By mindfully taking the perspective of my students, I can see situations through their eyes and be more responsive to their needs. Children learn how to build relationships by watching how we relate to them. By applying our own mindfulness to our relationships with them, we are teaching them how to do this at the same time.

Make Decisions Wisely

The culmination of the four skills described above supports the ability to make ethical and constructive decisions and carefully choose actions based upon them. Mindfulness supports this ability because it helps us see the situation as it actually is with openness and acceptance, rather than biased judgment. Since we can recognize and understand the perspectives of others and how they relate to our own, we are more able to respond in ways that support everyone's needs. We can teach this skill by modeling our own mindful awareness applied to the decisions we make involving our students. We can also apply our own mindful awareness to supporting our students' conflict resolution process by coaching them and sharing perspectives with them.

For example, once a conflict arose in the playground over a dump truck. Sam was grabbing the truck away from Kelly, and they were screaming at each other. As I approached, I heard Kelly say, "I had it first! You can't take it from me." Getting down to their eye level, I gently asked them to let go of the truck so I could hold it. I said, "I'm going to hold the truck until we can solve this problem so no one gets hurt." Then I asked, "Kelly, can you tell me what's happening?" Kelly said, "I was playing with the truck and Sam came over and grabbed it." Sam screamed, "But I had it first! I was getting a stick to put in it and Kelly just took it!" Kelly yelled back, "But you left it!"

"Let's all take three deep breaths so we can calmly solve this problem," I suggested. I reminded them how to do this and they quickly calmed down. "I can see that you both want to play with this truck. Sam had it and went to get a stick and Kelly took it. I can see that both of you are very upset about this situation. Kelly, can you tell me what you think about how Sam feels?"

Kelly sighed and said, "I guess he is mad that I took the truck, but he left, so I thought he was done with it."

"Sam, can you tell me how Kelly feels?" I asked.

Sam said, "I guess he didn't realize that I was still playing with it."

Finally I asked, "Can either of you think of a solution that you will both be happy with?"

Sam said, "Kelly, do you want to play with me? I was putting sticks in the truck and making a fort over there." Kelly responded with enthusiasm. I handed Sam the truck, and he and Kelly ran off to the fort.

To provide this level of coaching and support, I needed to apply mindful awareness to the situation, to observe what was happening without judgment, and to monitor my emotions and tendency to problem solve for my students. I didn't know who really had the truck first, and I knew that if I arbitrated the situation without engaging them in the process, their learning would be limited.

A Basic Compassion Practice for Adults

Often those of us who care for others find that we have difficulty giving ourselves the self-care we require to have the energy to keep on giving. Self-care requires noticing what you need and recognizing the value of giving yourself what you need. Generating compassion for others can begin with generating compassion for ourselves. This simple practice combines breath awareness and the body scan and involves filling your body with compassion with each breath, until your body is full of compassion. Once this occurs, you can breathe compassion into the world as if it is overflowing from your body.

I suggest that you begin by lying down for the practice. If you need to, you can bend your knees to relieve any tension in your lower back. You can lay your hands on your lower belly or by your sides. Take a moment to feel the weight of your body on the floor and then shift your awareness to your breath, feeling the sensation of the air filling your lungs and then leaving your body with each breath. After a few minutes of breath awareness, imagine that your body is surrounded by a circle of compassion. Imagine that this compassion is warm, kind, and nurturing. If it helps to imagine this compassion as having a color, feel free to add this to your image of compassion. Once you have your body surrounded by this warm, loving compassion, imagine that with each breath you inhale compassion, filling your lungs with it. When you exhale, imagine that the compassion in your lungs fills your entire body through your circulatory system. You can imagine that it's somehow linked to the oxygen in your lungs, and the compassion enters your bloodstream with each exhalation along with it. Imagine that the compassion fills your body starting with your feet and slowly filling your calves, knees, thighs, hips, abdomen, chest, arms, shoulders, neck, and head, until your entire body is full of compassion. Once your body is full, with each breath, imagine that your body radiates compassion, spreading it outside your body. As you continue to breathe, imagine that the circle of compassion continues to grow larger with each breath, encompassing your loved ones and other people and animals in your life. When you first learn this practice, you may choose to end it here. After gaining additional experience, you may wish to try extending the circle of compassion.

Continue to imagine this circle of compassion growing to include people you don't know and even people you may not like or agree with. See if you can expand the circle of compassion to include all living things, both plants and animals. Finally, see if you can expand the circle of compassion into the future, to encompass people, animals, and plants yet unborn.

A variety of other compassion practices are available through apps and websites (see appendix). One common practice is called loving-kindness practice, or *metta*, which involves generating and extending feelings of care and well-wishes sequentially to yourself, a loved one, a neutral person for whom you have no strong feelings, and a person for whom you have uncomfortable feelings. After you have practiced the breath awareness practice, the body scan, and the compassion practice described here, loving-kindness practice is a recommended next step.

In this chapter we have covered the basic background information you need to understand how to integrate mindful awareness and compassion into your teaching. We learned what mindfulness is and two simple mindful awareness practices. We learned how mindfulness and SEL are related and a simple compassion practice. Now you are ready to begin learning mindful awareness and compassion practices for kids.

However, developing and maintaining your own mindfulness practice routine is required to deeply embody mindfulness so you can scaffold the practice for your students. I strongly recommend participating in ongoing professional learning in the form of retreats, engaging in evidence-based programs such as Mindfulness-Based Stress Reduction (MBSR; Kabat-Zinn, 2009) or programs specifically developed for teachers such as the CARE, CALM (offered by CREATE for Education) and SMART (offered by Passageworks) programs. Contacts for these organizations are located in the appendix. My first book *Mindfulness for Teachers* (Jennings, 2015a) contains valuable tips for cultivating your own mindfulness and how to apply it to enlivening teaching. Finally, I recommend reading any of the many books listed in the appendix to support your ongoing learning and personal development.

PART II

Mindful Awareness Practices for Kids

How to Calm Down
and Pay Attention

As Ohio Congressman Tim Ryan (2014) reminded me during a talk he gave at the University of Virginia, we are constantly telling our kids to calm down and pay attention, but we never tell them how. At its most fundamental, mindful awareness practices for children can teach these simple skills, calming down and paying attention. Young children are developing cognitive, emotional, and behavioral self-regulation skills, and their ability to self-regulate depends upon their age and maturity. The development of the prefrontal cortex of the brain plays a critical role in these functions. As we learned in Chapter 2, EFs and self-regulation skills are the mental functions that help us to focus attention, plan, remember instructions, and successfully manage multiple tasks, all essential to school and life success. These functions help us filter distractions, prioritize tasks, control impulses, and achieve goals.

Certain activities and experiences can promote or inhibit the development of these functions. Trauma and toxic stress can distort EF development as the brain tries to adapt to extreme threat. Children can become hyper-aroused and hypersensitive to threat, or spaced out and dissociated. These distortions are adaptive in that they help the child deal with situations that are too emotionally harrowing to tolerate. But they interfere with the functions critical to learning in the school environment. Simple activities that build self-management and attentional skills can support children's recovery from trauma (Jennings, 2019).

Two simple mindful awareness practices help children learn these critical skills. In *Thrive! The Compassionate Schools Curriculum* (Jennings & Harris, 2018), we call them calming and focusing. Calming involves taking slow, deep, mindful breaths, and focusing involves directing attention to the sound of a bell. We teach the students about what we call anchor points, the center of the chest and the lower belly. We invite them to put one hand on their chest and one hand on their belly when they are engaging in these practices, so they can feel the sensations of their breath and can focus their attention on the body during these practices. We introduce the idea that just like a boat's anchor, anchor points help us stay steady.

Both of these activities intentionally involve practicing these skills outside the context of formal academic learning, when the stakes are low. The activities train the skills without the complications of other learning content. In this way, the skills are developed in isolation, but also the message that they are inherently important is communicated.

There are a variety of ways to engage in these practices. First we will learn the basic instructions for each practice, and afterward I present a variety of extensions and modifications that you can use and adapt to meet your own needs.

Calming

While the research is quite preliminary, there is evidence that the practice of taking slow breaths has beneficial effects on children's anxiety (Khng, 2017) and adults' mood and overall well-being (Perciavalle et al., 2016) by stabilizing the nervous system. When we take slow, deep belly breaths, our nervous system calms down, like turning down a thermostat.

The autonomic nervous system controls unconscious body functions such as heart rate, digestion, and the stress response. The sympathetic branch of the system is involved in activating functions, such as increasing heart rate and blood pressure. The parasympathetic branch has the opposite effect, decreasing activation. The autonomic nervous system plays a vital role in allostasis, our ability to achieve and stabilize well-being (McEwen & Wingfield, 2003). When you consciously take slow deep breaths, your brain gets the message that the world is safe, and it activates the parasympathetic branch of the nervous system, making you feel calmer. In contrast, if you take shallow rapid breaths, or hold your breath, the sympathetic system is activated, associated with excitement or threat.

We can practice taking slow, deep mindful breaths when we begin to notice the sensations associated with the stress response, and it will calm us down immediately. When I begin to feel tension in my neck, shoulders, and jaw, I realize I'm beginning to get stressed out, and that's when I know I need to take some breaths. We can teach our students this simple practice. Once it becomes a routine part of the day, you can use it to help kids calm down in the midst of high emotions or conflict.

You can also use it to calm yourself in the midst of tough situations when you are teaching. Rather than trying to suppress strong emotions, you can model self-regulation for your students. First give your students an "I" message such as this: "When students are talking while I am giving a lesson, I begin to feel frustrated because the other students can't hear me." Then you can describe this feeling of frustration: "When I feel frustrated, I notice that my shoulders and neck get tense and I begin to clench my jaw." Next, model what to do to manage this uncomfortable feeling. "I'm going to take three mindful breaths to calm down, and I'd like you to join me so we can get back on track together." Engaging in modeling self-management in this way serves a dual purpose. It gives us a chance to calm down and teaches the skill of calming down at the same time.

Introduction to Calming

A wonderful tool to provide a concrete example of calming activity is something called a mind jar. This is simply a jar filled with water and glitter (see instructions in the resources section of the appendix including an eco-friendly alternative to glitter). To teach calming to your students, begin by showing the children a mind jar. "Look at this jar. Now watch while I shake it. What do you see?" The glitter is swirling around. "If I hold it still for a few minutes, what happens?" The glitter settles to the bottom of the jar. "Let's imagine that this jar is like our mind and body. Do you ever feel like your mind is spinning like the glitter jar? Do you ever feel like your body is all stirred up like the glitter in the jar? We are going to learn how to calm down our bodies and minds. If we can hold our body still and take three slow deep breaths, we can calm down, just like the glitter in this jar.

"First let's all sit up nice and tall. To practice calming, we need to use a muscle in our belly called the diaphragm. This muscle makes our belly expand when we take in a deep breath and contract when we exhale. Place your hand on your belly, and let's practice taking a deep breath. Don't strain. Just take in a deep breath of air, and then let it out. Let's take another one and try to make it a little bit slower. Now, as you take the next deep breath, see if you can feel the air as it is going into your nose and filling your lungs. You can also feel your belly rising and falling with each breath. What do you notice? What does your breath feel like?"

Take a few minutes to engage the students in reflecting on the experience of taking deep breaths. When they understand the concept and recognize the feeling of deep breathing, lead them in the formal practice.

"Now let's do the calming practice together. Make sure you are sitting in an upright posture. Not stiff like a board, but uplifted. Have you ever seen a puppet on strings? Imagine that you have a string on the top of your head that is pulling your head up, just a little bit. Now put your hands on your belly. If you want to, you can close your eyes. If not, just look down at the floor. Now, together let's take three deep breaths. One, bring the air into your body. Feel the air filling your nose and your chest, feel your diaphragm rise. Now exhale, letting the air out slowly. Two, breathe in again, feeling the air filling up, slowly and fully. Notice the feeling of the air entering your body. Then exhale slowly. Now let your breathing settle back to normal and notice how you feel. Three, take in one more slow, deep breath, feeling the air going in and your belly rising. When you're finished, allow your breathing to settle back into its normal rhythm."

Lead the students in a discussion about how their body feels after the three deep, calming breaths. Encourage your students to be expressive, noting how their bodies feel by describing sensations. If one says she feels calmer, ask, "What does calm feel like?" Here are some example discussion questions:

- Can you describe how your body felt when you were breathing in?
- How about when you were breathing out?
- Can you describe how your body feels now?
- Does it feel different than it did before the breaths?
- Can you describe how this kind of breathing is different than your regular breathing?
- How is it similar?

Extensions to Calming

There are many ways to extend the understanding of calming into other learning activities. Depending upon the age of your students, you can adapt these extensions to increase or decrease their level of difficulty.

Hoberman Sphere

An easy way to help students understand deep breathing is to use a Hoberman sphere to provide a concrete example of expansion and contraction. A Hoberman sphere is a geodesic sphere toy made of plastic that can be

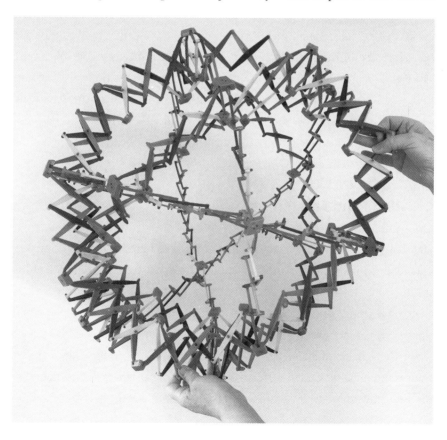

expanded and contracted by pulling it apart or pushing it together. Introduce the sphere to your students by showing them how it can expand and contract, just like our lungs. You can use the sphere to guide the practice of inhaling and exhaling by expanding and contracting the sphere along with instructions for breathing.

Encourage students to focus their eyes on it, rather than closing their eyes, if you'd like. Sometimes young children have difficulty closing their eyes, because of their curiosity and their lack of inhibitory control, a type of EF that is still developing. Having something to focus their eyes on can help them attend to the activity. The children can also lead the breathing practice with the sphere. You can give each student a turn to lead the practice, or invite a student who is disengaged to be the leader, a dependable way to captivate interest.

Creating Mind Jars

One simple extension is to lead your students in creating their own mind jars. Baby food jars work great for this activity. It helps to canvas your parents for jars in advance so you have enough for each student. See the detailed instructions in the appendix for making mind jars. Once each student has their own mind jar, they can use it to help themselves calm down when they need to. Jars can be labeled with each student's name and be stored somewhere accessible. When children need to calm down, they can get their mind jars and practice breathing on their own. This will also help you monitor how your students are feeling throughout the day.

Vocabulary Building

Depending upon your students' age, you can introduce them to a rich vocabulary around feeling states. Begin by reminding the students about the calming practice and the mind jar activity. Holding a jar, shake it up and ask the students to describe what they see. They may say that the glitter is swirling around or going crazy. "When you are feeling like the glitter, what other words could you use to describe the feeling?" Some words children may come up with include excited, irritated, frightened, anxious, worried, stressed out, frantic, stirred up, mad, and so on. Write all the words down on a chart as the glitter settles. Then ask your students, "Now that the glitter has settled, can you think of some words to describe this feeling besides *calm*?" Students may generate words such as still, quiet, peaceful, tranquil, resting, and so on. Throughout the day, ask the students to assess situations using the vocabulary by asking questions such as, "How did the character in the story feel? Which words from our word chart can you use to describe her feelings?"

Creative Writing

To develop students' understanding further, include calm as a theme in creative writing activities. For example, you can invite them to generate similes using the sentence stem "as calm as," or you can use sentence stems to prompt them, such as, "calm is . . ." Introduce other poetic devices such as alliteration, personification, imagery, rhythm, metaphor, and repetition. You can invite them to write stories titled "A Calm Day" or "A High-Energy Day."

Self-Assessment

One way to help children learn self-awareness and self-regulation is to teach them how to assess their own energy level by tuning into their bodies. Students can create their own "energyometer" that they can use to gauge their energy level (see directions in the appendix). You can begin by showing them how to gauge the level of swirling in the mind jar. Create a demonstration-sized energyometer and introduce it to the class with the mind jar: "Here's a new tool for us to use when we need to calm down. We'll call this our energyometer. Just like a thermometer that we use to measure the level of temperature, the energyometer measures our level of energy." Shake the mind jar. "When our bodies and minds are swirling like the glitter, we are experiencing a high level of energy, and we can indicate it on our energyometer like this." Slide the indicator to the top, indicating a high level, and slowly draw down the indicator as the glitter settles.

"Now I'm going to shake the jar just a little bit. Who can show us on the energyometer how much swirling the jar is showing now?" Invite one child to set the indicator to represent the level of swirling in the jar. At a later time, when students are engaged in something, take a moment and ask the class about the level of energy in the room. Ask someone to set the classroom energyometer to indicate the level. Help the students gauge their own level of energy using their own energyometers and mind jars. Over time, students will develop the ability to notice their energy level and their need to calm down. They will also learn that different energy levels are good for certain activities. For example, before silent reading time, you can ask, "During silent reading time, what level of energy is best? Can someone show us this on our energyometer? Do you think we need to take come calming breaths right now so we have the right energy for silent reading?" In contrast, when it's time for recess you can ask, "During recess, what level of energy is best? Can someone show us this on our energyometer?"

Swirling Activity

Young children love to spin, and you can invite your students to pretend they are the pieces of glitter in the jar and spin and swirl together, being careful not to bump into one another. Once the glitter begins to settle, you can say, "The glitter in the mind jar is beginning to settle. Show me what this looks like. Can you settle slowly to the ground like the glitter?" Eventually the children will all be lying on the ground, settled like the glitter.

Blowing

To encourage students to take deep breaths, practice blowing. Demonstrate how to take a long, slow inhalation through your nose and then blow out strongly through your mouth. Invite the class to practice this together. Next invite your students to blow something like a pinwheel or bubbles. You can engage your class in creating a pinwheel as an art project (see instructions in the appendix).

Breathing Buddies

A wonderful way to help preschool and kindergarten children practice deep breathing is to use a breathing buddy. This can be a stuffed toy, a beanbag, or a rock that the children place on their lower bellies. As they take deep breaths, they give their breathing buddy a ride on the waves of each breath. Making breathing buddies is a fun activity. Even very young children can make their own beanbags if they are introduced to simple sewing activities sequentially. Children can find rocks and decorate them with a face to make their own buddy. Instructions for these activities are in the appendix.

Focusing

Every day we are bombarded with a deluge of sensory stimuli, both internal and external. As we learned in the discussion of the Wheel of Awareness, we can intentionally direct our attention to sensory stimuli as named on the rim of the wheel. Young children are just beginning to develop their attentional skills, which are essential for learning. Attention is involved in all information processing, including determining which internal and external stimuli require a response and should be singled out and processed.

The ability to select stimuli from this complex web of constantly changing multisensory activity is determined by the characteristics of the stimuli and a variety of factors, including the child's motives, interests, cognitive strategies, and developmental stage. In order to learn a new skill, a child must be able to identify and attend to important aspects of the activity and to discriminate differences and similarities in dimension and quality. Maria Montessori understood how to help children develop attention by isolating elements of the environment to simplify the activity and to reduce distractions. Her sensory materials were designed so that only one element was different to cultivate attention and make sensory discrimination easier. For example, her famous pink cubes are a set of 10 blocks that increase in size from 1 centimeter cubed to 10 centimeters cubed. They are all the same pink color. Dimension is their only difference, and young children can easily focus on this one attribute to sort them by size.

The ability to select stimuli from the environment for further processing is also related to what information ends up stored in memory. If a child does not attend to important information, it will not be later recalled, or may be recalled without enough detail or specificity to be useful. There are different ways that specific stimuli are selected for attention. The selection process can be automatic, which occurs when our attention is oriented by something novel, like a loud noise. The process can also be active, as in the case when we are intentionally looking for something. This is called selective attention. Another dimension of attention is arousal. In order to attend, we must be alert and able to sustain our focus long enough for information processing and learning to occur. As we discuss the focusing activity, keep in mind these four components of attention: orienting, selective attention, arousal, and sustained attention. Research has proven the benefits of practicing attentional skills for both children and adults. Indeed, sustained attention therapies can improve children's ability to delay gratification, which is also associated with many positive outcomes across the life span (Murray, Scott, Connolly, & Wells, 2018).

In focusing practice, we use a chime as an auditory target for sustained attention because it has a built-in sustain in the form of resonance. To practice focusing, you will need a chime or a bell that resonates for a long time.

Woodstock Chimes makes some single chimes mounted on a wooden stand that work well and are inexpensive. I prefer not to use a bell or chime that has religious significance, because it can give the impression that the practice is not secular, which is especially important in U.S. public schools (Jennings, 2015b).

Before introducing the practice to your students, introduce the bell, holding the chime in one hand and the striker in the other as follows: "Today I'd like to introduce something new to our classroom. This is a chime that is mounted on a piece of wood. This is the stick that we use to ring the chime by gently hitting it. In a minute I'm going to ring the chime and I invite you to listen carefully to the sound. Are you ready?" Hit the chime lightly but loudly enough for it to ring for some time. Lead the students toward recognition that the chime resonates over time by asking questions like these:

- Can you describe what you heard?
- What did you notice about the sound?
- Did it sound the same the whole time?
- How did it change?
- Why do you think the sound changed?

Say, "I'm going to ring it again, and this time let's see how long we can hear it. I'm going to use a timer to see. When you don't hear the sound anymore, raise your hand." Using a timer on a smartphone, check how long it takes for the last student to raise his or her hand.

Once the students are familiar with the bell and understand how the sound resonates, you can introduce the practice: "Now we are going to practice focusing our attention on the sound of the chime. I invite you to close your eyes or look down at your table or the floor. When I ring the bell, focus your attention on the sound and keep focusing on it until you don't hear it anymore. Then see what else you can hear and try to hear the sound that is the farthest away."

When your students are ready, ring the chime. Give them plenty of time to sustain their attention. When you think they have had enough time, ask, "What did you notice? What did you hear?"

Don't be surprised if they come up with things that you didn't hear, because their hearing acuity is much better than ours. Engage in a discussion about what they heard. You can write down what they share on chart paper each day and see what is similar or different. Depending upon the location of your school, children may hear a wide variety of sounds including building noises such as the heating, cooling, or plumbing systems, people walking and talking in the hallways or adjoining classrooms, children playing outside, traffic noises, nature sounds, and so on.

Extensions to Focusing: Selective Attention

Once your students are able to sustain their focus on the sound of the chime, you can introduce a selective attention practice. This involves listening to a variety of recorded sounds. For example, I made a recording of the sounds in my backyard in the summer. At this time, there are a variety of bird songs and sounds of crickets, frogs, and dogs barking along with traffic noises. This recording worked well for this exercise.

Begin by telling your students that you will be introducing a new focusing practice: "Today we are going to learn another way to practice listening. I have made a recording of the sounds in my backyard. I invite you to close your eyes and listen to it." Turn the recording on for about a minute. After you turn it off, ask the students what they heard. "Next we will listen again, but this time I will tell you which sound to focus on." Turn the recording on again. "Listen for the sound of the dog barking in the distance. See if you can tell how many times the dog barks." To do this, children need to selectively attend to just the sound of the dog barking in the midst of other auditory stimuli, strengthening their selective attention skills. Practices like this can also reduce self-focused attention and strengthen self-regulatory abilities. Another way to practice selective attention is to introduce your students to listening to classical music and picking out specific instruments. A great introduction to listening to orchestral music is Sergei Prokofiev's *Peter and the Wolf* with narration for children.

Focusing Attention on Other Sensory Stimuli

Once your class is easily sustaining focus and can selectively attend to various auditory stimuli, you can focus on stimuli for other senses. Next I describe various practices that involve other senses and that also incorporate learning content.

Focusing on a Candle

Back in the days when I was still teaching, I used a real candle to focus on. Today, this is likely not possible (nor safe), so I recommend you use an electric candle instead. There's something about the flickering of a candle that attracts visual attention, because our nervous system is hyperresponsive to visual movement and changes in light intensity (Yantis, 1996). You can introduce the flameless candle as part of your daily calming and focusing practice. "Today we are going to focus on something new, a candle." Show the students the candle and place it in the center of the circle. "This is a flameless candle. It flickers like a flame, but it's electric. After we do our calming breaths, I invite you to focus your eyes on the candle and notice what you see." Once they have stared at the candle for a minute or two, you can open a discussion about what they noticed about the candle.

Focusing on a Lava Lamp

Like the candle, a lava lamp can attract and sustain attention. Introduce the lamp to your students. "This is what's called a lava lamp. Today we will use it for our focusing practice. See if you can figure out why it's called a lava lamp." Allow the class to focus their vision on the lava lamp for a minute or two, then open a discussion about what they noticed and why they think it's called a lava lamp.

Focusing on Nature

Orienting and sustaining attention on features in the natural environment can be thrilling for children. When I was teaching, we used to take field trips to various nature preserves to observe nature. Sitting on a hillside overlooking San Francisco Bay, I invited my students to focus on one element of the panorama at a time. "I invite you to practice focusing as we look out over the bay. Let's begin by focusing our attention on a bird. Choose a bird and see if you can focus your eyes on it." A variety of seabirds were flying around picking up fish from the bay and diving and splashing in the water. After a few minutes, I said, "Now I invite you to shift your focus to the boats on the water. Pick out one boat and see if you can keep your eyes on that one boat until it moves out of sight."

I would continue suggesting various elements of the scene to focus on. Once my students were good at this, I would invite one of them to lead the practice when we were out on a field trip. Depending on their ages, children can be encouraged to identify specific elements in nature such as types of flowers and trees, shapes of leaves, types of birds, and other wildlife. I was always amazed at the things my students noticed that I didn't even see.

There are likely many other ways to practice building attention, and I encourage you to use your creativity, especially when it comes to bringing attention to curricular content. One of my favorite activities was to introduce my preschoolers to vertebrate animals, one at a time. Each year I would begin with the fish. Rather than telling them all about the fish, I placed the fishbowl in the center of the circle and invited my students to focus on the goldfish (named Goldie, of course). Just like the other focusing practices, I invited them to focus their eyes on Goldie and watch her carefully. We sat in complete silence for several minutes while the students were entranced by our goldfish as she made lazy in circles in the water.

After a few minutes I asked, "What do you notice about Goldie?" The students shared a number of interesting observations. For example, Sean asked, "How can Goldie breathe under water?" This gave me an opportunity to point out her gills and explain that fish are adapted to breathing under water. Alma said, "Fish swim differently than we do." I asked, "How so? Tell me more." Alma: "They don't have arms and legs like we do, but they have these other wiggly things on the sides of them and their tail wags them around." This was a great opportunity to give these parts of the fish names and explain how they work.

Mindful Eating

We can apply our mindful awareness to the sense of taste by practicing mindful eating. I suggest that you introduce this practice with strawberries, because they are easy to eat and have a richness of flavors in each bite. Be sure to check if any of your students are allergic to strawberries before you do this. It's fine to use another fruit if strawberries are an issue. Prepare enough strawberries so each child can have one. Wash them carefully, but leave the stem and leaf, if they have them attached.

Introduce the practice: "Today we are going to practice focusing with a strawberry. Would someone like to help me pass out napkins and straw-berries? Be sure that you only take one so everyone can have one. Once you have your strawberry, place it on your napkin until we're ready to begin the focusing practice."

Once the children all have a strawberry, you can begin the practice. "Let's begin by focusing our eyes on the strawberry. Look at it carefully and see what you notice about its shape, color, and texture. Now gently pick it up by the stem and look at it more closely. Turn it around and see if the color and texture are different on the various sides of the strawberry. Now hold it up to your nose and smell it. What does it smell like? Hold it up to your ear. Can you hear anything? Now let's touch the body of the strawberry very gently so it doesn't leak juice. Hold it gently in your hand and touch it with the fingers of your other hand. What does it feel like? Is it warm or cold? Is it smooth or rough? Now let's try licking it, but don't take a bite yet. What does it taste like? Now take a tiny bite, but don't swallow it. Let it sit in your mouth and notice if the taste changes and what happens in your mouth. When you are ready, you can swallow the piece of strawberry and take another small bite. Does this bite taste any different? How so? Can you savor the taste of the strawberry?"

Continue with this questioning as they finish eating the strawberry. Let them know that this is a different way of eating. You can introduce the word *savor*, which means to perceive a taste or a smell with relish. Tell them that when they savor their food, they can enjoy it more. Encourage them to try focusing the next time they eat a meal. Ask them to report back to the class their experiences with focusing on eating.

Focusing on Touch

One fun way to practice focusing is by using touch. In my classroom I had a velveteen bag where I kept a variety of items to practice focused touching. I had a larger stash of items stored in a cupboard and would circulate them to maintain the novelty of this task. I introduced it as a circle time activity, but sometimes left it out in the classroom for children to choose to work with alone or in small groups.

"Today we are going to focus our attention on touch. Here's a bag with some things in it, and I'm going to see if I can figure out what they are, just by feeling them. I'm not going to look." Put your hand into the bag and feel around for one object. "I have one thing in my hand. It's round and cool. It feels like it's made of glass. I think it's a marble." Take the item out of the bag and show it to the class. "I was right! It is a marble. Who would like to try next?" The students can take turns reaching into the bag, focusing on one item with their tactile sense and trying to identify it without looking.

Another extension involving focused attention on touch is called Take Five. Students trace each finger of one hand starting with the base of the thumb and ending at the base of the little finger. They inhale as they trace up each finger and exhale as they trace down, resulting in five breaths. They are instructed to feel the sensations of both the touch and breath. This activity can help with behavior management because it involves the use of both hands, especially helpful when a student's high energy involves touching others inappropriately.

In this chapter, we have learned the two basic mindful awareness practices for preschool and elementary children, calming and focusing. I recommend that you begin the school year by incorporating them into your daily routine at the beginning of class and to support transitions. Once your students build this habit, it becomes part of the classroom culture, and the children know when they need to calm down and pay attention and can practice these activities intentionally when necessary. While the extensions can breathe new life into the calming and focusing routine, I recommend that they be introduced slowly. Don't overwhelm your students with too many types of activities at once. As you become more comfortable with leading these activities, consider ways to incorporate them into your curricular content as much as possible. This will help your students engage more deeply in learning. In Chapter 4, we will explore ways to teach applications of mindful awareness to self-care.

Caring for My Body

Returning to our discussion of the Wheel of Awareness, the focusing practices described in Chapter 3 involved the five physical senses. In this chapter, we will learn mindful awareness practices that involve the sixth sense—inner bodily sensations. I like to call this listening to the body. In this chapter, I focus on sensations associated with hunger, thirst, and sleepiness, the vestibular sense (balance and where the body is in space), and the stress response.

Being able to listen to the body is key to lifelong health. When we listen to how we are feeling inside, we can determine what our body needs and can give it what it needs. Children are particularly attuned to the body because they haven't begun living life in their heads, like we adults do.

Sensations of Hunger and Thirst

When we began working on *Thrive! The Compassionate Schools Curriculum* (Jennings & Harris, 2018), we embarked on an extensive review of the literature on healthy eating skills for children. We discovered that many of the attempts to improve childhood nutrition through education had failed, primarily because young children have little control over what they eat. The one approach that has been found successful is called eating competence, developed by Ellyn Satter, a registered dietitian, family therapist, author, trainer, publisher, and consultant. An internationally recognized authority on feeding children and eating, she developed the Satter Feeding Dynamics Model and the Satter Eating Competence Model and has conducted research to test these models and to help professionals and parents apply them to supporting children's nutrition (Satter, 2008). Eating competence involves building a good relationship with food. This means having a positive attitude about food, being flexible with eating, and trying new foods. It also involves recognizing the bodily sensations associated with eating and digestion such as hunger, thirst, satiety, and fullness.

In Chapter 3, I introduced mindful eating, one element of eating competence. In this chapter we will learn how to introduce our students to the inner bodily sensations related to food and how to recognize the nourishment our body needs.

Noticing Thirst

Let's face it, children don't drink enough water when they are at school, and when they become dehydrated, they can become cranky and unsettled. A study involving a large, nationally representative sample of children showed that inadequate hydration is a prevalent health problem among U.S. children, especially among boys, non-Hispanic blacks, and Hispanics (Kenney, Long, Cradock, & Gortmaker, 2015). Drinking adequate water can improve children's performance on cognitive tests and providing 10–17 ounces of water to children during the school day improves cognitive performance. However, this is only a fraction of the approximately 56 ounces of water recommended. Being able to recognize thirst is vital to self-care. Often we confuse sensations of hunger and thirst, eating when we really need water. I recommend finding a way to provide water bottles to each of your students or ask parents to purchase one for them. Be sure to recommend bottles that are not breakable and don't leak. Having their own bottles helps them maintain hydration and gives them the responsibility to notice when they are thirsty. It will likely help them concentrate and be less irritable. Children may not notice when they start to become thirsty. This can make them susceptible to becoming dehydrated, which is why learning to notice thirst is an important skill for children.

At the beginning of the school year, include the water bottle in your system of routines and procedures, which are covered in more detail in Part III. When you introduce the bottle, also explain how important it is to drink water when you are thirsty. A good time to explore the feeling of thirstiness is after recess, when children have been running around and are likely dehydrated.

"Today we are going to learn how to focus on our body's feeling of thirst. What does it mean to be thirsty? What does your body need when you feel thirsty?" Children will likely say that their body needs water when they are thirsty, but if they don't you can prime them with questions like these: "Do you need food? Do you need sleep? Did you know that your body is composed of 75% water?" (Note that this is higher than for adults, which is closer to 60–70%.)

"Are you thirsty right now? Often we get thirsty when we've been running around outside, especially when it's hot. Let's take a few minutes to focus on how our bodies feel. Try closing your eyes and feeling your body. What do you notice? If you think you are thirsty, raise your hand. Now take a sip from your water bottle and check in on your body again. Does it feel any different? Do you need more water? Go ahead and drink as much water as you think you need. Each time that you take a sip, notice how you feel. Stop before you feel too full of water."

Show the students where the water bottles will be stored and review the procedures for using them. To end the lesson, say, "When we check in with our body to see how it feels and what it needs, we call this listening to our body. If we listen, our body will tell us what it needs, and taking care of our bodies is very important to our health and well-being."

During this lesson or at another time, you can introduce fun facts about how our body uses water. For example, we constantly lose water from our body when we go to the bathroom, when we sweat, and when we breathe. If we don't drink enough water, we become dehydrated. You can show the students a grape and a raisin as an example of dehydration, so they can see what happens to a grape when all the water dries out of it. Water helps our body in many ways. It helps our blood carry nutrients to all the cells in our body and it carries away waste. It helps us cool our body when it's hot. All drinks and food contain water, but drinking plain water is best for us. We can survive for up to 50 days without eating any food, but only a couple of days without water.

Noticing Hunger

Recognizing signals of hunger is an important skill associated with healthy body weight and psychological well-being. Children often confuse the feeling of hunger with other uncomfortable feelings such as boredom and frustration, so learning how to identify the sensation of hunger is especially important for them. Research has identified several specific sensations associated with hunger. First is the hunger pang, when one feels a kind of emptiness or hollowness in the stomach. Another is the stomach rumbling that signals hunger. The third is sensations associated with low blood sugar, which can include fatigue, light-headedness, and general weakness (Kenney et al., 2015).

A good time of day to introduce noticing sensations of hunger is right before lunch, when your students are likely hungry. Before you excuse them to go to lunch, introduce a new body listening activity.

"Today we're going to listen to our body in a different way. Today we're going to notice if we are hungry. What does it mean to be hungry? What do we need when we are hungry? Let's check in with our body to see if we can feel what hunger is like. Let's close our eyes and feel our body." Allow the children to listen to their bodies for a minute or two. "What do you notice? Do you think you are hungry? How do you know? What does hunger feel like?"

Engage the students in a discussion about the sensations of hunger. See if they identify any of the sensations noted in the research cited above. Reinforce this recognition of hunger by acknowledging the sensations of hollowness (pangs), rumbling, and weakness.

"When we listen to our body and notice we are hungry, it's a good time to eat a meal or a snack. It's a good thing that it's lunch time! As you eat your lunch today, see if you can practice mindful eating and notice how your body feels after you eat a little food. When you return, let's check in again and see if our body feels different."

Noticing Satiety

Satiety is the feeling of fullness after eating. This sensation plays an important role in managing how much we eat. How can we recognize satiety? A number of bodily signals create the sensation of satiety. Signals that are linked with specific networks in the brain respond to the sensory experience of the food, the feeling of expansion in the stomach, and hormones that are released during the digestion and absorption of food by the body. These hormones can give us a feeling of contentment. We can feel the stomach filling up before the satiety signals reach the brain. This is why it can be helpful to eat slowly and wait for a bit to see if we are still hungry.

When the students return from lunch, invite them to listen to their body to see if they feel any different after eating. "What does your body feel like now after you ate lunch? Do you notice any different sensations in your body or mind? Are you full now? How do you know?" Engage the students in a discussion about the sensations of fullness. If they are old enough, you can introduce the word *satiety*; if not, just use the word *fullness*. See if they identify any of the sensations noted by the research cited above. Reinforce this recognition of satiety by acknowledging the sensations of a full stomach and a sense of contentment or satisfaction. If appropriate, this is a great time to introduce how the body uses food for growth, energy, and health.

Sleep and Rest

Depending upon their age, children often fight the feeling of sleepiness and may become irascible when they get overtired or overstimulated. Research is learning more about the importance of sleep and children's need for adequate sleep. Sleep is especially important for children, as it has a direct impact on their mental and physical development. We now know that during sleep our brains engage in a process of eliminating toxins, critical to well-being (Xie et al., 2013). During the preschool years, children often need an afternoon nap, even if they don't fall asleep. Throughout elementary school, taking short periods of rest can help children maintain their energy level throughout the day. A good time to notice sleepiness is after lunch or later in the afternoon. I recommend that you begin by reading a book about sleep such as *The Napping House* (Wood, 2015), an engaging book about a family of animals that take a nap together on the bed with a granny and child. Invite your students to lie down on the floor or a yoga mat. Invite them to close their eyes and notice how they feel.

"Let's listen to our body to see if we're sleepy. What does sleepiness feel like? Are you sleepy now? How do you know if you are sleepy?" Give them about five minutes to rest quietly. If you'd like, you can lead them in the body scan activity that you learned in Part I, or turn on some soothing music for them to listen to. Afterward engage them in a discussion about the feeling of sleepiness.

"How do you feel now? Are you sleepy anymore? How do we know that the granny and the child in the story are sleepy? What about the cat and the dog? Sleeping is very important for our health, especially our brain's health. When we sleep, our brain gets a good cleaning!"

The Stress Response

When children learn to recognize the sensations associated with the stress response, they are more able to use the calming practice proactively, before they become overwhelmed and less able to self-regulate. When we feel threatened, physically or psychologically, our body goes into high gear to give us the strength we need to survive. Hormones and neurotransmitters trigger the sympathetic nervous system to prepare us to fight or run. These reactions happen quickly and automatically, but we can notice sensations in our body that give us clues about how we are feeling. One way to explain this to children is by teaching them about the brain and how it responds when we feel threatened. Dan Siegel (2009) suggests teaching them about the hand model of the brain. Begin by holding up your hand for your students.

"Imagine that your hand is a model of your brain. The wrist is your spinal cord that sends signals throughout your body from your brain. Your thumb is your limbic system, where your brain processes emotions. There is a small part of the limbic system called the amygdala, which is like an alarm that goes off when it feels threatened. The fingers are the brain's shell, or cortex. It surrounds the limbic system like this." Curl your fingers over your thumb as indicated in Figure 3.

"The prefrontal cortex is located in the forehead here." Point to the front of the middle knuckles of the first three fingers. "This is the part of the brain

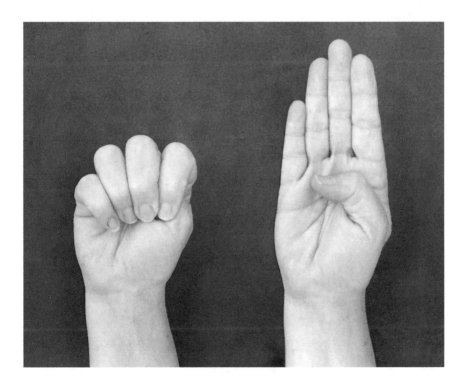

that helps us pay attention and think clearly. It helps us make plans and good decisions. Usually it helps keep our emotions under control, because it is connected to the limbic system and can tell it to calm down. But sometimes when we get really stressed, angry, or scared, we flip our lid, and the prefrontal cortex is no longer in contact with the limbic system." Raise up the fingers from the thumb as shown in Figure 3. "When this happens, the amygdala sends an alarm that triggers the stress response to help us fight, run quickly, or freeze. When we feel stress like this, it's hard to think clearly, and sometimes we do or say something that we later regret. But with our calming practice, we can take three deep breaths and calm down, so we can put the lid back on, and our prefrontal cortex remains in charge. Then we can make a good decision about how to handle the situation."

This is a very simple metaphor of a much more complex process, but children find it interesting, and it gives them a rudimentary understanding that they can work with. It helps to provide an example of a situation that might trigger stress: "For example, imagine that you arrived at school and found out you had a test that you had completely forgotten to study for. This might trigger your fear and your flight-or-freeze response, and you may find that you flip your lid. How might you feel if this happened? Can you describe this feeling of fear and dread? Where do you feel it in your body? What else do you notice?"

Children might describe a sick feeling in the stomach as the digestive system shuts down to prepare them to run, or a shivering sensation as the blood drains from the extremities as they freeze. "When we notice these feelings, we can recognize that we are feeling stress and fear. Since we can't do anything about forgetting to study, all this stress is not really helping us. In fact, it might make it harder for us to learn. So, this is the time when we want to use our deep breathing to calm ourselves down, so we can get our prefrontal cortex back in charge of our brain."

Be sure to offer other examples of fear and anger so they can explore the various sensations that they feel during these emotions. For children exposed to trauma and toxic stress, it helps to use a story about a character, rather than asking them to reflect upon hypothetical feelings that might trigger strong reactions (Jennings, 2019). Once they learn to recognize the bodily sensations of the stress response, they are much better prepared to self-regulate, and their emotions don't take them by surprise. They are also better at understanding others. When a friend flips his lid, a child is much better at recognizing that her friend is experiencing the stress response, and she can help him put his lid back down by encouraging him to take some slow deep breaths.

In this chapter, we learned ways to teach students to apply mindful awareness to self-care. With practice, children can learn to listen to their body so they know how they feel and what they need. They can become more aware of hunger, thirst, the need for sleep and rest, and the stress response. All these skills are critical to the SEL skills of self-awareness and self-management and can prepare our children to attend to their well-being for the rest of their lives.

5

Mindful Movement

In this chapter, I introduce simple mindful movement activities that help children develop poise and coordination. They also help students build balance and proprioception, the ability to notice where your body is in space. Returning to the Wheel of Awareness, the sixth sense can be mindfully explored with movement. Focusing attention on the body as it moves through space or as it balances in place helps children develop concentration and coordination.

From the moment they are born, children want to move around like the other people in their lives. Beginning with the jerky, uncoordinated movements of early infancy, it's clear that they are born with a formidable drive to develop coordinated movement. Just watch a 6–9-month-old as she tries to propel herself across a room, using a combination of rolling and scooting until she finds herself stuck in a corner. This drive to move continues throughout childhood and plays a vital role in human development across the life span (Payne & Isaacs, 2016). During the preK–5 years, children are still developing and refining both fine and gross motor skills. Maria Montessori recognized the importance of supporting motor development and intentionally considered it in the design of her learning materials (Lillard, 2005). We can draw upon her ideas for inspiration as we introduce mindful movement activities to children. First we will explore ways to apply mindful awareness to gross motor activities, followed by activities to promote mindful fine motor coordination.

Gross movement involves the large muscles such as those of the thighs and upper arms. These muscles help us walk, run, jump, and skip. In contrast, fine movements involve the small muscles of the hands, fingers, and forearm critical to finger and hand movement. Activities such as handwriting, drawing, sewing, typing, or playing a musical instrument are considered fine motor skills. Although movements are often classified as either fine or gross, all movement involves the coordination of both groups to some degree. For example, handwriting involves the coordinated activity of the fingers, hand, and forearm, but also requires the upper arm to place the hand while writing.

We can bring mindful awareness to any type of movement. As I type these words, I can bring my mindful awareness to the feeling of my fingers hitting the keys of my laptop. I can feel the smoothness of the keypads as well as the weight of the laptop on my lap. I can also bring mindful awareness to gross motor activities such as walking, focusing my attention on feeling the weight of my body shifting from one foot to the other. In the next section, we explore activities to apply mindful awareness to gross motor activities.

Mindful Gross Movement

Children love to move, and today schools provide ever fewer opportunities to build motor coordination. Sitting for long periods of time is not good for any of us, and it helps to take a break and move around periodically. You can use such times to teach your students to bring mindful awareness into their movement. These activities are not intended to replace recess and physical education but to provide opportunities for children to build awareness of where their body is in space and how to move consciously and with coordination.

Centering

This is a very simple activity that helps us feel present and centered in our body. Invite your students to stand up and tell them that you are going to teach them how to be centered. "Let's all stand up. Take a few minutes to shake out our body. Let's shake our head. Now let's shake our arms, now our legs, then our whole body. When you've had enough shaking, let's let our body settle into a standing posture with both your feet on the floor, parallel and about hip width apart." Demonstrate the posture, showing them what you mean by *parallel* and *hip width*.

"Now feel the weight of your body pressing your feet against the floor. Can you feel your weight on your feet? Let's shift our weight a little bit, but be careful not to shift too far because we don't want to fall down. First let's shift from left to right. Now let's shift a little back and forth. Now let's try to find the center where our weight is balanced between both legs. Everything has a center of gravity. Gravity is the force that keeps us on the earth." This understanding can be incorporated into your science curriculum, which can include a more thorough discussion of gravity, balance, and the center of gravity. It helps to show the students a plumb line and connect it to the understanding of gravity and the center of gravity.

"Our center of gravity is located in the lower belly. This means that the force of gravity is pulling your body down toward the earth from this point. Let's imagine that there's a plumb line connected from our center of gravity to the ground, pointing straight down toward the center of the earth. You might want to bend your knees just a little bit. See if you can feel yourself centered and grounded. Now let's take our calming breaths. This is a way we can bring calmness and stability to our whole body." This activity can prepare children for other movement activities such as mindful walking, lining up to go outside or inside, or getting ready to play a physical game. It can also be helpful for children (and adults) who are anxious about performing or speaking in front of an audience.

Mindful Walking

After introducing centering, you can introduce mindful walking. It helps to introduce this practice where you have enough space to form a circle and walk around in a circle. "We have been practicing our centering activity, and today we are going to add walking to this practice. Let's begin by getting centered." After completing the centering activity as described above, continue introducing mindful walking: "When we walk, the weight of our body shifts from one foot to the other. We can feel this weight also shift across the sole of our foot." Demonstrate slow walking, noting how your weight shifts from one foot to the other. "When we practice mindful walking, we pay attention to the weight of our body as it shifts from one foot to the other. Let's all turn toward our right and make a line in a circle. Begin walking slowly so you can feel the weight of your body shifting from one foot to the other." Continue walking in this way for a few minutes.

Do not become alarmed if some of the children get silly and fall down. This is a perfectly normal response to this activity. Simply keep going and reinforce the focus on the weight of the feet on the floor. With time and practice, children will improve. This type of walking can become part of your classroom routine, when you need your class to walk in line. We have found that this activity makes teachers' lives much easier, because it explicitly teaches children how to focus their attention while they are walking.

There are a variety of extensions of mindful walking. Maria Montessori invented an activity called walking on the line. In this activity, children carefully walk around a circle made with tape on the floor. This requires a bit more balance than simple mindful walking, because the children must put one foot directly in front of the other and still maintain their balance. Preschool children love this activity, and I noticed how much my students improved during the school year. With older children, you can move this activity to a low beam or a curb, and then raise the beam as their balance and coordination improve.

The Bell Activity

Another activity derived from Montessori's ideas involves walking on a line while holding a small bell without letting it ring. For this activity, you need at least one small hand bell. Demonstrate the activity by holding the bell in front of you by its handle with your thumb and two forefingers. Slowly walk around the circle, being careful not to let the bell ring. Then invite the children to try, one at a time. If you have more than one bell, you can invite several children to walk around the circle with the bells at one time. Do not be surprised if the bells ring, intentionally or accidentally, and do not admonish them when this happens. It takes time and practice for them to begin to focus on the task and be skillful and self-regulated enough to inhibit the impulse to ring the bell.

This activity can be modified to involve carrying other things that require balance, such as a pitcher of water or a stack of blocks. You can use your creativity to come up with challenges for your students, or you can invite them to create challenges for themselves. With time, children develop gracefulness and more intentionality in their everyday movements.

Yoga

Developmentally appropriate yoga is an excellent way to practice mindful movement with children, and I encourage you to learn simple yoga postures that you can practice with your students. The appendix includes a bibliography of yoga books and curricula for children, including how to access *Thrive! The Compassionate Schools Project Curriculum* (Jennings & Harris, 2018), which is freely available online. This curriculum offers a compendium of developmentally appropriate lessons that integrate yoga, SEL, various mindful awareness practices, and mindful eating.

Mindful Fine Movement

Mindful awareness can also be applied to fine motor skills. Holding a pencil and writing are two of the most important motor skills for school success. These skills are more difficult than we often imagine and often require opportunities to prepare eye-hand coordination with other, less challenging activities, especially in preschool and the early grades. Without such support, young children can form habits that are difficult to overcome and that make writing difficult, uncomfortable, and even painful.

A variety of activities can help prepare the child's hand to hold a pencil properly and can also cultivate mindful awareness. For example, stringing beads or macaroni on a necklace is a simple activity that involves holding a small item and the end of a string in a manner that strengthens the hands and fingers and builds eye-hand coordination. You can create opportunities for children to create patterns with different colors, which also builds cognitive skills. To introduce such an activity as a mindful awareness practice, demonstrate the activity mindfully, carefully showing the children each step of the process with little talking or explaining. Think about the lesson as a mindful awareness activity itself and recognize that by demonstrating the activity mindfully, you are scaffolding mindfulness for your students. When they have an opportunity to engage in the activity themselves, they are more likely to engage their own mindful awareness. If they do not, it's perfectly fine. The intention is not to force them to practice but to create the conditions that invite mindfulness into the experience.

Other activities that support hand strength and eye-hand coordination in preparation for writing include peg boards, puzzles with pegs, sewing activities, and using various utensils such as eyedroppers, tweezers, scissors, tongs, spoons, and ladles. Using a cotton swab to polish silver or a cotton ball to polish a shoe also builds these skills. Once young children have the manual dexterity to hold a pencil correctly and write, we can move on to mindful writing and drawing activities.

Bell Activity 2

The same bell or bells can be used in a different way to develop fine motor coordination. During this activity, invite students to stand in a circle, close enough so that each student will be able to pass the bell to his neighbor, around the circle. Begin the practice with centering. Remind them to feel the weight of the body on the ground and to find their center of gravity.

"I'd like to invite you to set an intention together. The intention is to pass this bell around the circle without letting it ring." Let the students know that if it rings, it's really no big deal, but that we want to give ourselves a challenge. Also tell them that this is a voluntary activity and they can step out and watch if they feel uncomfortable. "Let's take a few minutes to consider what we need to do to be successful. Any ideas?" They may suggest that they need to be calm and focused. If not, you can bring this up. If they don't mention it, be sure to tell them that it helps to be silent. When everyone is ready, you can begin passing the bell to the person on your right.

Children ages 8 and up can do this quite easily, although they may get silly and lose focus. If that happens, simply note what has happened. "Oops, we just lost our focus. That's okay because we know how to calm down and focus. Let's try again." When everyone has settled, start again. When the bell gets around the circle once without ringing, celebrate. "We did it! We got the bell around the circle without letting it ring. Congratulations!" Then lead them in a discussion, reflecting on what they noticed during the activity. Often students notice how nervous they feel as they wait for the bell to come to them. You can ask, "What does it feel like to be nervous? Can you think of a simile?" Children also report that they noticed that they had to work together and be careful when they passed the bell so their partner could grasp it without making it ring. Sometimes students figure out that they can hold the metal part of the bell so that it can't ring. However, sometimes this strategy backfires, because it actually makes it more difficult to pass without letting it ring.

I love this activity because it involves so many opportunities to explore mindful awareness around the Wheel of Awareness. We can notice how we mindfully focus our vision on the bell as it moves from person to person. We can notice that our sense of hearing becomes accentuated as we anticipate ringing. We can feel the bodily sensations associated with nervousness and relief as the bell approaches and moves past us. We can notice our mind as we worry that we'll be the one person who rings the bell. We can recognize the mindful awareness of the relational sense as we work together on a shared intention and help each other be successful.

When your students are good at this, you can increase the level of difficulty by adding more bells to the activity. "We are getting really good at the bell activity. I think we're ready for the advanced version. What do you think?" Start passing around one bell, and then, after a few seconds, start a second bell in the opposite direction. Continue adding bells to the activity by starting a new one alternating in each direction. Eventually students will find that they have two bells coming to them at the same time and they need to navigate how to pass them. Although this is a bit of a challenge, it makes the game more interesting, and kids love it. After the bells have been circling for a few minutes, you can invite them to stop and let them ring the bells. Then engage them in a similar discussion, reflecting on how they felt and how the advanced version feels different than the basic version of the activity.

Mindful Drawing

There are a variety of ways to engage students in mindful drawing. I suggest beginning with something related to what you are studying. As I mentioned earlier, when I introduced vertebrates, I brought an animal into my classroom, and we practiced mindfully looking at it. The first animal we studied was the fish, and I brought a goldfish named Goldie in a bowl to class and we spent some time mindfully watching her. Later I set up a station where my students could mindfully draw a picture of her. The bowl was on a table where the children could sit and watch her. I made colored pencils and paper available and encouraged them to draw a picture while they mindfully watched her. Before I created this station, I demonstrated how to mindfully draw, first placing the fishbowl back in the center of the circle and placing a small table in front of me with colored pencils and paper.

"Today I will introduce a lesson on how to focus on Goldie and draw a picture of her. First I will spend some time watching her." Quietly and mindfully watch the fish for about a minute or so. Then pick up a pencil and begin to draw the outline of the fish. Allow yourself to draw spontaneously, and don't worry about what it looks like. When adults draw pictures extremely well, it can sometimes be intimidating to children. Just create the general shape of the fish, like your students might do. Show the students the shape you made, but you don't need to say anything. Then say, "Now I'm going to focus on the fish again, to see what else I should draw." Again, mindfully watch the fish for 30 seconds to a minute. Then pick up another pencil and draw some other parts of the fish, such as the eye. Hold up the paper and ask your students what they notice about what you drew. Continue in this way until you draw all the parts of the fish, including the gills, the scales, the fins, and the tail. If you wish, you can also draw anything else in the bowl, like seaweed or rocks. Show the students where the activity will be located in the classroom and tell them they can focus on Goldie and draw a picture when they have time. You can also do this as a whole-group activity. However, often it's difficult to see the details of the fish unless you are close to it.

As you can see, you can use mindful drawing to support learning by helping your students focus their attention on the details related to the learning activity. Mindful drawing can involve seasonal activities. For example, in the fall, students can collect leaves and do mindful drawing of their vibrant colors. In the spring, flowers make excellent subjects for mindful drawing. Form drawing is another way to practice mindful awareness that also directly prepares children for writing. You can buy books with a variety of forms, or you can use stencils that students can trace.

Mindful Writing

When children are first learning to write letters, they often need help learning the movements they need to form the letters. One way to support this learning and practice mindfulness is an activity I call rainbow name tracing. Take a piece of butcher paper and write the child's name in big letters across the page, showing the child where each letter starts and ends. After you write the name, make red dots at the places where the letters begin and green dots at the places where they need to change directions. Then give the student a set of colored markers and invite her to trace her name in rainbow colors, one color at a time. Remind her to direct her focus mindfully on the movement of her hand as she traces her name in each color. This activity is helpful for young children just beginning to write but is also great for supporting an older student who is having difficulty writing. It builds fine muscle coordination along with attentional skills.

Once students have a good understanding of how to write individual letters and they are beginning to read, they can practice penmanship by tracing. One of my students' favorite tracing activities involved tracing a favorite poem or song. I would write the poem on lined paper with a black marker and laminate it. Then my students would take velum paper and carefully trace the letters of the poem. In this way, they would develop writing skills and also become familiar with the words in a poem or a song. They would also become familiar with the rhythms and structures of the rhymes and phrases.

In this chapter, we have explored a wide variety of mindful movements that can build both gross and fine motor skills. In Chapter 6, we learn ways to teach children to appreciate and cultivate feelings of kindness and compassion for themselves and others.

Cultivating Kindness
and Compassion

Compassion has been defined as a complex cognitive, affective, and behavioral process involving the awareness of suffering, feeling empathy, emotion regulation to manage strong feelings that come with empathizing with a person suffering, and the motivation to do something to help (Goetz, Keltner, & Simon-Thomas, 2010). This system evolved out of our need to care for our young, who come into the world so underdeveloped and in need of constant care and attention. Compassion likely extended to other loved ones and community members because it was adaptive. Humans have always needed one another to survive, and social bonds increase survival potential.

Today we are seeing the understanding of compassion extend beyond our immediate in-groups of family, friends, and people who have similar beliefs and appearance. There is a growing recognition of the interdependence of human beings, animals, and all of life. When global events such as nuclear war or climate change have the potential to extinguish life on a massive scale, we become more aware that we are all in the same boat and must work together to survive—all of us. We also become more aware of the suffering of other living things: animals facing extinction and environmental degradation, forests being clear-cut, coral reefs dying en masse (Ricard, 2015).

At the same time, the increase in the rate of social change makes it difficult to predict the future. Human beings evolved under conditions of relative stability. In our small social groups or tribes, we knew what was expected of us and we learned how to survive in one location. We rarely traveled far, and social and environmental changes were gradual. The rapid increase in change is frightening. When we can't predict what our lives will be like within the next few decades, it's difficult to prepare ourselves and our children for the future. Fear promotes the return to tribalism that we see mounting today (Hobfoll, 2018). To overcome this tendency, it is essential that we learn to manage our fear, build resilience so we can adapt to rapid change, and generate feelings of compassion for our fellow human beings, even those who are quite different from us. This transformation, along with cultivating compassion for all life on this planet, has become an urgent need for our survival (Turkovich, n.d.).

Children are very sensitive to these issues and are very responsive to encouragement to cultivate and extend compassion and kindness to others. Even very young children understand the value of kindness and compassion. In experimental settings, toddlers demonstrate altruism by helping an adult when they recognize a need (Warneken & Tomasello, 2007). We can cultivate and build upon this inclination toward altruism by demonstrating and naming altruistic acts, such as basic manners and courtesy. We can encourage our students to reflect on how others are feeling when it is obvious they are hurt or unhappy, so they learn to recognize and empathize with another's suffering. We can teach students that you can disagree with someone and still be their friend. This is best done in the context of everyday problem-solving and conflict resolution processes, such as the example I provided about Kelly and Sam and their conflict over the toy truck in Chapter 2. When faced with an unhappy peer, giving students opportunities to consider appropriate action can support their budding altruism. I suggest that teachers (and parents) refrain from rote demands for apologies. When an adult says, "Say sorry" or "What do you say?" with the expectation of an apology, children can mistakenly learn that an apology is all that is necessary to resolve a conflict. A better approach is to ask them to consider what the other person needs or how they might help the person feel better. This gives them an opportunity to seriously consider the unhappy peer's feelings, develop empathy, and express compassion and kindness without adult pressure. It provides an opportunity for students to consider how best to repair the harm that they have caused another.

Mindful Listening

When we bring mindful awareness to listening, we can imagine that we are a warm and friendly receiver that holds space for the person talking with openness and acceptance. Often when we listen, we tend to think about what we're going to say in response, rather than giving the person talking our full, undivided attention. To introduce your students to this practice, you can begin by having students read their writing to one another in pairs. This can be a poem or a short story. Begin by making a connection between the focusing practice and mindful listening.

"We've been practicing focusing our listening on the chime. Today we're going to focus our listening attention on one of our classmates who will read us a poem. Everyone will have a partner, and one person will be the reader and the other will be the listener. Then we'll switch and each person will have a turn to read or listen." Before they engage in this activity, provide the appropriate guidelines about giving constructive feedback and remind them about these guidelines.

Elicit reminders about how to focus on the chime. "Who can tell me how we listen to the chime?" If they don't come up with these guidelines, you can remind them to be very still and silent, focus their full attention on the bell, and listen to it until the sound is over. "We're going to do something similar in this poetry listening activity, only this time we're going to listen to our partner read."

Tell them that it helps to sit side by side, rather than face to face, and to look down, rather than at their partner. "The practice is to silently listen to the other person, without saying anything. Just listen with your full attention, just like listening to the bell. There is one important difference though. The bell doesn't have feelings, and your partner does. So bring kind and friendly attention to your partner. At the same time, you can notice how your body feels as you listen. What does your body tell you about the poem? How does it make you feel? Does it elicit something visual in your mind's eye, your imagination? After your partner has read the poem, write down how you felt as you listened. During this time, let's all remain silent. The reader can also write down some thoughts about how it felt to read a poem to this partner. Then you can switch roles and do the same thing again."

After they have each had a turn, they can engage in a dialogue about the experience. We have found that it helps to have them both take turns and do the writing reflections before the discussion because it helps them recall and savor the experience. After all the dyads have completed the activity, engage the students in a large group discussion about their experiences asking questions such as these:

- How did it feel to read your poem to your partner as they listened mindfully?
- How was that different than it usually is when you read or talk to someone?
- How did it feel to listen to your partner this way? It's okay if it felt a bit strange, because we don't usually listen like that.
- What did you notice about your thoughts and feelings as you listened to the poem?

Kind Mind

There are a variety of contemplative practices that are intended for generating feelings of care and compassion for others. A basic adult practice is called loving-kindness practice, or *metta*, in Pali, an ancient Indo-Aryan language.

In this practice, one generates feelings of goodwill toward oneself, a loved one, a neutral person, and a challenging person. A complete description of this practice can be found at the end of this chapter.

Kind Mind Practice With Self

This practice can be simplified and introduced to children. It helps to keep the practice as concrete as possible by starting first with the practice of generating feelings of kindness toward themselves and their bodies. In the *Thrive! Compassionate Schools Project Curriculum* (Jennings & Harris, 2018), we call this the kind mind practice. Introduce the practice by reminding them how important it is to take care of their bodies. You might want to refer back to mindful eating and the other previous activities related to self-care, especially listening to the body.

"It's important for us to be aware of what our body needs and to take good care of it by eating good foods and getting exercise and sleep. Today we're going to learn a new practice called kind mind. This is a way to take care of our body from the inside. When you listen to your body and treat it with kindness, it will help you make healthy choices."

Invite the children to sit up nice and tall and put their hands on their anchor points so they can notice how they are feeling. "Today we are going to practice a kind mind toward ourselves. This is a way to teach our minds to be kind to ourselves." As they sit with their hands on their anchor points, invite the students to repeat these words, either together out loud or silently at their own pace, taking one slow deep breath between each one so they can allow the feeling of caring for themselves to sink in.

"May I feel happy.

"May I feel healthy and strong.

"May I feel peaceful.

"How does it feel to say these words to yourself? Sometimes it may feel a bit strange, but that's okay. This might be because we're not used to practicing a kind mind toward ourselves, but this is a great way to teach our minds to do this."

Encourage your students to come up with other short phrases of kind words to share with one another. You can incorporate this into a language arts activity such as poetry writing.

After you have introduced the basic practice, you can incorporate it into a mini–body scan practice. Invite the students to lie down on a yoga mat or blanket. Invite them to spend a minute or two noticing the rising and falling of each breath.

"We learned how to practice the kind mind with ourselves. Now we're going to practice giving our whole body kindness. Take a moment to think about how you would talk to a good friend who is unhappy and needs your help. How would you feel? What words would you use? Let's apply this feeling to giving our bodies the same kind of care and kindness.

"Let's notice our feet and legs. How are they feeling? Do you notice the weight of your legs and feet on the mat? Let's bring kindness to our feet and legs by saying some kind words to them in your mind: 'May my feet and legs be healthy and strong. May I take good care of my feet and legs.'

"Next notice your belly and see how it feels right now. Is it full or empty? Comfortable or uncomfortable? Quietly, in our minds, let's say some kind words to our belly: 'May my belly be healthy and strong. May I take good care of my belly, feeding it with healthy foods.'

"Next notice your hands and arms. Can you feel the weight of your hands and arms lying on the mat? Quietly, in our minds, let's say some kind words to our hands and arms: 'May my hands and arms be healthy and strong. May I take good care of my hands and arms. When I take care of my hands and arms, it helps me use my hands and arms to care for others.'

"Next I invite you to notice your chest, your lungs, and your diaphragm as they move with each breath. Notice how your breath feels and in your mind say some kinds words to your lungs: 'May my lungs be healthy and strong. May I take good care of my lungs, being grateful for each breath I take that gives nourishment to my body.'"

Allow time for the students to come out of the practice, slowly coming back up to a seated position. Engage the students in a brief discussion about their experiences with the kind mind practice.

Kind Mind Practice Toward Others

After the students have had an opportunity to practice kind mind with themselves and their bodies a few times, you can extend the practice to others. Begin by reminding them about the mindful listening practice. "Today we will practice kind mind with a partner, offering kind words, just like we offered them to ourselves. We will practice mindfully listening as our partner offers kind words to us. As you listen, notice how you feel and what thoughts arise as you listen. Remember to listen with openness and kindness for your partner and yourself."

Once the students all have partners, ask them to decide who will be the listener first. For this activity, invite them to look at their partner. It may feel a bit strange, so acknowledge this, but tell them that this is an experiment, to see how we feel when we send and receive kind words. Have them try looking at one another to practice. Let them know that if it's too uncomfortable, they can look down. If the students laugh or giggle or show other signs of discomfort, acknowledge that what they are doing is new and that it's normal to feel silly at first.

Once they are ready to begin, invite the speakers to repeat the kind phrases after you one by one. "May you feel healthy and strong. May you feel happy. May you feel peaceful." Encourage the students to gently place their hands on their hearts to remind them that their kind thoughts come from the heart. Between each phrase, take a moment to check in to see how they feel.

As in the mindful listening practice, you can invite them to write down how they felt after each turn. After both of them have had a turn, invite them to have a dialogue about the experience. Then guide the class in a group discussion about the activity using the following prompts.

For the listener, ask, "How did it feel to hear the kind words from your partner?"

For the speaker, ask, "Did you feel heard? How did it feel to say kind words to your partner?"

Remind them that it's okay if it felt strange because it's not something we usually do, but maybe it also felt good too. Remind them that communicating with friends is a skill that takes practice. Sharing kind words can help us build strong friendships.

Grace and Courtesy

Maria Montessori included lessons in what she called grace and courtesy. These are very simple lessons in how to perform simple acts of kindness and use good manners. We often expect our students to come to school with this knowledge, but they actually can use help learning and understanding simple manners. These lessons may vary depending upon the age of your students. For preschool children who are relatively new to group settings like school, begin the school year introducing simple manners like saying "please" and "thank you," common greetings, walking past someone without pushing, and introducing a new friend. Each of these can be presented in a large or small group setting, and you can demonstrate them with another adult or student.

Please and Thank You

"Today we are going to learn some very important words we need to use regularly in our classroom. These words are *please* and *thank you*." Ask the students when you might use the word *please* and when might you use the words *thank you*. Set up a common situation where these words are appropriate. For example, while passing out a snack to the class, you can introduce this idea: "I'm going to pass out crackers. Each student can have two. I will offer you a cracker by saying, 'Would you like a cracker?' What do you think you should say if you want a cracker?" Prompt them to say, "Yes, please." Offer a tray or basket of crackers, giving them a chance to take two.

"What should you say after you take the crackers?" Prompt them to say, "Thank you." "What should you say if you don't want a cracker?" Prompt them to say, "No, thank you." "What if it's not snack time and I'm not passing around crackers, but you're really hungry and would like one. What would you say to me?" Prompt them to say, "May I have a cracker please?"

Greetings

"When we see someone we haven't seen for a while, we greet them with friendliness and kindness to let them know we are happy to see them. There are several ways that we can do this. One way is to shake hands. I will show you, but I will need a partner." Invite a student to help you demonstrate shaking hands. "When we shake hands, we stand facing our partner and we look at them in their eyes. We put out our hand like this to offer it to the other person. The other person takes our hand, and we gently shake it like this." Take turns practicing shaking hands with a few other students and then invite the students to practice with each other. "Who can think of another way to greet a friend?"

Depending upon your students' cultures, they may suggest a fist bump, a high five, or a hug. You can demonstrate each of these the same way, being sure to emphasize that these are invitational gestures. For example, we don't just grab someone and hug them. Demonstrate how we open our arms and offer a friend a hug. If the friend doesn't reach back, you can always change the offer of a hug to an offer of a hand. You can encourage your students to practice this so they understand the signals of their partner and can respond accordingly.

Excuse Me

"Sometimes we need to walk by someone who is in our way. To do this with grace and courtesy, we need to say, 'Excuse me,' and wait until they move out of the way." I will demonstrate how to do this. Invite a student to block a pathway in the classroom with his back to you. "When he is in my way, I can say, 'Excuse me,' so he knows I need to walk past him. Then he can move out of the way so I can pass." Take turns practicing this with a few other students and then invite the students to practice with each other.

Introductions

"Today we are going to learn how to introduce a friend to someone." Invite two students to help you demonstrate. "Jane, I would like to introduce you to my friend Sally. Sally, this is Jane. Jane can say, 'Nice to meet you, Sally.' And Sally can say, 'So nice to meet you, Jane.'" Take turns practicing this with a few other students and then invite the students to practice in groups of three.

We have learned several activities and practices for cultivating compassion and kindness in our classroom. However, I can't overstate how important it is for us to engage in adult practices to cultivate our own compassion. We are the models for kindness and compassion, and if we are not kind, our students won't be either. It's not always easy to remember this in the midst of our hectic days and when dealing with challenging situations. The loving-kindness practice can help us build the capacity to cultivate and sustain kindness and compassion.

A Simple Adult Loving-Kindness Practice

This is a simple practice that you can engage in to cultivate and extend your own feelings of compassion and kindness to yourself and others. Find a quiet place to sit and begin by taking three long, slow, mindful breaths. Then allow your breathing to settle into its natural rhythm. Focus your attention on your breath, noticing the sensations of the air going in and out of your lungs, just as we practiced in Chapter 1. Spend a few minutes focusing on your breath to allow your mind to settle. Then begin to offer yourself these kind words silently in your mind: "May I enjoy well-being, happiness and peace," or you can simply imagine yourself as well, happy, and peaceful, whichever works best for you. Spend a few minutes repeating this process, offering yourself well-being, happiness, and peace while generating feelings of care and kindness for yourself.

Next shift your awareness to a loved one. This can be a partner, a parent, a child, a friend, or even a pet. You likely have many people in your life that may fit into this category. For this activity, choose one for now. Once you have chosen this person, imagine them in your mind's eye, or simply think about them while mentally offering them kind words: "May you enjoy well-being, happiness, and peace." Repeat these words or imagine your loved one as well, happy, and peaceful and generate feelings of kindness and care for this person.

Next shift your awareness to a person for whom you have no strong positive or negative feelings, a neutral person. You likely have many people in your life that may fit into this category. For this activity, choose one for now. Once you have chosen this person, imagine them in your mind's eye, or simply think about them while mentally offering them kind words: "May you enjoy well-being, happiness, and peace." Repeat these words or imagine this person as well, happy, and peaceful and generate feelings of kindness and care for this person.

Next shift your awareness to a person for whom you have some uncomfortable feelings. This may be someone who is a bit difficult or frustrating in some way. Don't choose a person for whom you have very strong uncomfortable feelings, as it may make the practice too difficult at first. Pick someone who is mildly frustrating. Once you have chosen this person, imagine them in your mind's eye, or simply think about them while mentally offering them kind words: "May you enjoy well-being, happiness and peace." Repeat these words or imagine this person as well, happy, and peaceful and generate feelings of kindness and care for this person.

After a few minutes, return to focusing on yourself, offering yourself kindness with the words, "May I enjoy well-being, happiness, and peace" or imagining yourself as well, happy, and peaceful, generating feelings of kindness and care for yourself. After a few minutes of practicing this, allow your awareness to settle back to your breath for a few minutes.

PART III

Cultivating a Mindful Classroom

Mindful Awareness
of the Classroom
Environment

By bringing a mindful eye to our classroom environment, we can create a warm and safe space that supports the efforts described in the previous chapters. In this chapter, you will learn how to optimize students' learning to engage in mindful awareness practices by considering multiple dimensions of the physical and psychological environment. You will learn how to apply mindful awareness to observing and designing your classroom and how to provide space for students to give themselves time to regulate strong emotions.

The Importance of Environment

During the 15 years I spent supervising student teachers as part of a teacher preparation program, I learned how important the classroom environment is to promoting prosocial behavior and learning. I observed student teachers in their placement classrooms once a month and provided them with mentorship support for the entire school year. Over time I became very adept at sensing the quality of the classroom environment and recognizing factors that are conducive to student well-being and learning. I approached each observation as a mindful awareness practice—watching what was happening moment by moment with an attitude of openness and curiosity. It became clear that the quality of the classroom environment and interactions plays a critical role in student learning. These interactions occur between teacher and student, student and student, and teacher/student and environment.

The classroom environment is both physical and psychological. The physical environment involves the layout of the classroom furniture, what is posted on the walls, windows, lighting, and wall colors. The psychological environment is the classroom climate: the general mood, attitudes, standards, and tone that we feel when we are in the classroom. A positive classroom climate feels safe, respectful, welcoming, and emotionally and instructionally supportive. In contrast, a negative classroom climate can feel chaotic, scary, and hostile. These two dimensions of the classroom environment, physical and psychological, work together to support student learning.

Optimizing Student Engagement in Mindful Awareness Practices

When introducing calming and focusing practices, it helps to have a space where there is room for the class to sit together on the floor in a circle. If you have room in your classroom to do this on a regular basis, it is ideal. Visual distractions and noise can make it difficult for students to attend to the practices, so I don't suggest trying to teach it in a room where other activities are going on simultaneously. Large open rooms such as the cafeteria or gym may also be distracting, because they feel too open. Students are used to engaging in very different activities in these rooms and may find it difficult to settle down. The cafeteria is loud and chaotic when students are present, and children are used to running around in a gym.

I have found that enhancing the peacefulness of the classroom during practice can help set the mood. I liked to turn the lights off and whisper to direct my class to walk mindfully to the circle and sit down for practice. Even in the most quiet and peaceful spaces, some students will find it difficult to calm down and pay attention, so it helps to be patient and offer alternatives to those who aren't ready, and you need to make space for this. One choice can be for a student to sit in the book corner and quietly look at a book. Another can be to lie down on a blanket and take a rest. Over time, these students may choose to join the class and engage in the practices.

Mindfully Observing

Practicing mindful awareness can support our understanding of our classroom climate and its impact on our students' learning. It can also help us cultivate and maintain a classroom environment that supports our students' ability to cultivate mindful awareness and promote learning. To bring a mindful eye to your classroom, spend a few minutes mindfully exploring the classroom at a time when no students are present. Look at the space through fresh eyes, seeing it as your students do. Get down to their eye level. Sit on the floor and look around the room. What do you notice? How do you feel? Does any feature jump out at you? Does it feel spacious or cramped? Now move to another spot in the room and sit down again. Look around and check in to see how you feel. Imagine being a student in this room. Does it feel safe and comfortable? Or busy and confusing? Then, at a time when your class is busy working independently, do it again. Sit down on a small chair at their level. Look around and notice how the room feels and how the students are interacting with each other and the environment. This practice of mindfully observing your students in the classroom can provide important insights into how the classroom environment is supporting or inhibiting classroom interactions and student learning.

Withitness

One day I was observing a preschool classroom. The students were busy working on various activities in learning centers, but it was loud and a bit chaotic. Both teachers were sitting on the floor separately focused on helping individual children, and it didn't appear that either of them was keeping an eye on the whole class. Two girls were building a house out of blocks and began arguing about how to construct the garage for a toy car. Their argument became heated, and one girl grabbed a block away from the other, yelling, "No, this block goes on the top!" Surprisingly, neither of the teachers seemed to notice this altercation.

A few minutes later, I saw a boy begin to climb onto the kitchen area counter to look for supplies for his art project. Again, the teachers didn't see this happening. Because the child was in a dangerous situation, I immediately went over to him and asked him to get down from the counter. "What are you looking for?" I asked. He told me he needed more glue for his project. I said, "When you need something, you should ask the teacher to help you. It's not safe to stand on the counter." He quickly got down, went to the teacher, and asked for help. This was a clear example of mindlessness. Had at least one of them been alert to what was happening around them, neither of these situations would have escalated as they did.

Jacob Kounin (1970), one of the first researchers to study classroom management, articulated a construct called he called "withitness," the ability to be aware of everything that is happening in the classroom and to proactively respond to situations before they become management issues. In the classroom context, withitness is the application of mindful awareness while teaching. After the observation, I told the teachers what I had observed and gave them tips for being more mindful of what was happening in the classroom. When coteaching, make sure one teacher is always monitoring the entire class. This involves sitting or standing in a position where you can see every part of the classroom. To do this, both teachers need to check in with one another often so that if one needs to help a child, the other can take over. My assistant teacher and I developed simple hand signals to indicate that we needed to attend to one child so the other would keep an overview of the classroom. Teachers also need to keep attention on the entire class while focusing on one child or a small group. Part of this involves mindfully attending to the sounds around you and keeping some attention on the periphery of your vision. With time and practice, it gets easier to flexibly deploy your attention in this way.

Elements of the Physical Environment

Classroom layout, color, wall clutter, and lighting can optimize or detract from student learning. A study conducted in the UK to examine the impact of various environmental factors on student learning involved collecting surveys from 153 elementary classrooms from 27 very diverse schools and examining the performance of 3,766 students learning in those spaces (Barrett, Zhang, Davies, & Barrett, 2015). Researchers examined three types of physical characteristics of the classroom: stimulation, individualization, and naturalness. The most important finding is that physical characteristics of elementary schools have a large impact on learning progress in reading, writing, and mathematics, explaining 16% of the variance in students' overall progress.

The study found that naturalness, including light, temperature, and air quality, accounts for half of the impact of the environment on learning. Individualization, including ownership and flexibility, accounts for about a quarter, and the appropriate level of stimulation (complexity and color) accounts for another quarter. An important finding was that there are many minor changes that teachers can make to their classrooms that are easy to do and don't cost much.

The one element of the environment that has the single greatest impact on learning is lighting. Authors recommend as much diffuse, natural lighting as possible. Be careful not to cover windows with posters or artwork, keeping them as open and free as possible. High-quality artificial light is important when natural light is not adequate. Lighting emitting a higher color-rendition index and a fuller spectrum promotes well-being and learning (Fielding, 2006). If you are stuck with the hanging fluorescent lights found in many classrooms, you can find inexpensive standing lamps and use full-spectrum LED bulbs to improve your classroom lighting. Fresh air is also important to learning, so it helps to keep the space around windows clear so they can be easily reached and opened when the room becomes stale.

Individualization is another element research found to be important. This factor includes two dimensions: flexibility and ownership. You can support flexibility by clearly defining learning zones, such as learning centers, group work areas, and quiet areas. It helps to create at least one space where groups can work independently and still feel connected to the rest of the class. To reduce distractions, arrange the space so that focal points are away from the doors and windows. At the same time, we want to be able to have visual access to all parts of the classroom so we can monitor student activities. One way to ensure this is to create spaces using shelving that is low enough for an adult to see over, but high enough for the students to feel like they have some privacy. You can create a sense of ownership by making displays of students' work, providing each student with a cubby, desk, or other space of their own, and providing furniture that allows both choice and comfort and provides a variety of spaces and types of seating.

The third factor researchers found critical to learning is stimulation, which includes complexity and color. Researchers found that the relationship between level of complexity and student achievement was curvilinear. If the classroom was too busy or too sparsely decorated, achievement was negatively impacted. A medium level of complexity was found to be best. This included enough diversity of the floor layout and ceiling material to stimulate students' attention but presenting a degree of orderliness. The visual displays on walls were well designed and organized and did not cover more than 80% of the wall area. A similar result was found for color. Large brightly colored areas and empty white walls both had negative impacts on learning, whereas light-colored walls with one complementary wall in a bright color were most effective.

Elements of the Psychological Environment

Young children are very sensitive to the adult's emotional tone, and you have a huge influence on the psychological environment. Taking time to check in with yourself regularly when you are teaching can help you manage your stress. If you begin to notice that stress is arising, take a few slow deep breaths.

Teachers are often given the message both explicitly and implicitly that we are supposed to always be in control of our students. When we apply mindfulness to this common misunderstanding, it becomes evident that this is impossible. We cannot control our students, but we can control ourselves and the environment. The typical classroom environment has multiple dimensions that tend to trigger stress and emotional reactivity. First of all, everyone in the room is constrained to the room. Neither the teacher nor the students can leave without a negative consequence. This situation puts psychological pressure on everyone, especially if the classroom is overcrowded. Another dimension that can trigger stress is the lack of privacy. Teacher and students have no privacy, making it difficult to manage strong emotions. Typically, when we feel a strong emotion and we know it is inappropriate to express it, we tend to find a place with privacy to calm down, so we don't do or say something we may later regret. When you are forced into a situation where this is not possible, it adds to the stress because you must manage your emotions in the open. Among teachers, this tends to result in the suppression of emotional expression, which is harmful to our physical and mental health (Chang, 2009). When we keep these dimensions in mind as we design our classroom space, we can ameliorate them.

Usually we have no control over the fact that we are confined to the classroom. However, we can create a space that feels safe and emotionally comfortable, which will relieve some of the stress associated with confinement. We can also create minispaces that give children a sense of privacy. For example, we can use shelving to create a book corner and a peace corner, both places where children can go when they need some "time in." The peace corner is a place in the room where children can go when they need a break or to calm down. This is a cozy place with soft stuffed animals, pillows, and other comforting items. The peace corner can also house items that help children self-regulate such as squishy balls, fidget toys, and a mind jar.

Typically teachers begin the year by inviting the class to design the peace corner so it can meet their needs and they can feel ownership of the place. Invite the students to imagine a safe, comfortable space and to draw pictures of what would make it comfortable. Often teachers ask children to reflect on a space like this in their own homes. However, I don't recommend this practice because some of your students may not have such places in their homes. Indeed, some of them may not have a stable home at all.

Orchestrating
and Conducting a
Prosocial Classroom

Classroom management is often the most challenging aspect of teaching. Without good classroom management, it is difficult to engage in mindful awareness practices with your students. In this chapter you will learn how to apply mindful awareness to your classroom management, including routine practices such as introducing, reminding, and reinforcing expectations and establishing classroom routines and procedures to promote prosocial behavior and enhance student learning. You will also learn mindful approaches for addressing chronic behavioral problems.

Establish Mindful Routines

Young children thrive in environments where there is routine and consistency. Because they are just beginning to learn so many things, being able to count on a stable environment and consistent routines promotes safety and security. The simplest and most basic step in this process is to start the day and each transition with a brief calming and focusing practice, taking three mindful breaths and listening to the chime. Since the chime becomes associated with this practice, I recommend not using it to signal any other routines. Find another signal and save the chime for the focusing practice. When calming and focusing become part of the classroom routine, children learn to expect it and often ask for it when they need it. If teachers don't prepare their substitutes to maintain the practice when they are away, students will ask for it. It helps to have one or two students ready to lead the practice and to alert the substitute during such times.

Similarly, choose among the many mindful awareness practices introduced in this book to become part of your daily routine. For example, you can practice mindful walking to and from lunch each day. You can practice taking a few mindful bites silently at the beginning of a snack or a meal. Practice centering at the beginning of a physical activity or a performance. You will know best how to incorporate any of these activities into your particular classroom context.

Build Community

Build a supportive community of learners by engaging in activities where students get to know one another and begin to feel like part of a caring community that values learning. Introduce books such as those listed in the appendix that promote prosocial values, friendship, and community. Lead your class in the group activities described in Chapter 5. Promote healthy peer relationships by mindfully observing classroom interactions for any evidence of troublesome behavior such as bullying or rejecting. Research has found that when teachers proactively work to reduce the status extremes in their classrooms and support friendship building among children who seem isolated, children report a strong sense of peer community, and classroom interactions are more supportive (Gest, Madill, Zadzora, Miller, & Rodkin, 2014).

Get to know your students and their families. Know and understand the relevance of the demographics and diversity of your school and classroom. Understand families' cultural perspectives and issues related to equity. The understanding of appropriate behavior in various contexts is culturally determined. Engage in culturally responsive classroom management by learning what good behavior and misbehavior mean to your students and their families (Ladson-Billings, 1995). Are there issues at home that might be interfering with the child's learning and behavior? How can you partner with parents to help?

Formalize Expectations

Engage students in thinking about necessary classroom expectations based upon their own hopes and dreams for learning (Denton & Kriete, 2000). Ask, "Why do we go to school? What do you hope to learn? What dreams do you have for this year?" In response to these ideas, brainstorm what behaviors the students will need in order to reach their hopes and dreams, leading toward a clear understanding of a few basic expectations (e.g., rules) such as, respect one another; respect our learning materials; do our best work (Brady, Forton, & Porter, 2003). Be sure your students understand what each of these expectations means and link them to specific classroom procedures.

Explicitly Teach Procedures

Teach classroom procedures that encourage independence explicitly using interactive modeling (Denton & Kriete, 2000). This process involves clearly showing your students what you expect and having them practice the behavior. For example, when teaching your students how to sit in the circle for morning meeting at the beginning of the school year, start by asking them how they can apply the classroom expectations to this situation. "How can we respect one another at circle?" They will likely answer that they can make space for one another and keep their hands to themselves. Give them these tips if they don't come up with them. Demonstrate exactly how you expect them to sit (e.g., legs crossed, hands in their laps, still and quiet) and where (e.g., on the rug or circle). Next ask the students what they noticed. "What does it look like to sit in the circle? What does it feel like? What does it sound like?" Then ask one student to show the class how to walk to the circle and sit down. Then ask the students, "What does it look like, feel like, sound like?" The process of interactive modeling helps students embody these procedures and connect them to the expectations.

Complete this procedure for each of your classroom routines. It helps to begin the year with the most basic daily routines such as lining up, sitting in circle, using the bathroom, and using classroom materials. As the year progresses, you can add more routines as needed, following the same process.

Reinforce Expectations and Procedures

Bringing mindfulness to our teaching can help us be vigilant (but patient) and consistently reinforce expectations and procedures. Young children need time and practice to consistently enact expected behaviors. At the beginning of the year you will likely need to remind the students each time you begin a procedure. When students follow the procedures correctly, be sure to reinforce their appropriate behavior. For example, "I see you all sat down in the circle quietly with your legs crossed and your hands in your laps." Or, "I see you lined up quietly and respectfully with your hands to your sides." When they are off track, redirect them with comments such as, "Show me how we sit in the circle." Or, "Show me how we line up." Develop simple verbal and nonverbal signals and a "teacher look" to make reinforcement efficient.

When students' behavior does not align with classroom expectations, first remind, reinforce, and then redirect. Avoid nagging and reminding more than once. If this doesn't work, calmly and with a matter-of-fact voice, present a logical consequence that is related to the behavior. This might be one of three primary consequences: (1) you break it, you fix it; (2) loss of privilege; or (3) take a break.

For example, a student knocks a snack tray out of another student's hand. Ask the student to clean up the mess and offer to get a new snack tray for the student (you break it, you fix it). Or if a student is using art materials incorrectly and continues to do so after reminding and redirecting, say, "I expect you to respect our classroom materials. Take a break from the art area until you are ready to show me how to respect the glue" (loss of privilege). Create a space for taking a break in your classroom and introduce how it is to be used. This can be a chair set aside for cooling-off periods. It's very important that this chair not become associated with punishment. Punishment is intended to induce shame and can provoke resentment and power struggles (Jennings, 2015a). Introduce the take-a-break chair as a place students can go when they need to calm down and pay attention. You can include the practice of calming as part of the process of sitting on the chair. Use interactive modeling to show your students what to do during the break (Denton & Kriete, 2000).

Be the Change

Build your own social and emotional competence by practicing mindful awareness, reflection, and self-monitoring throughout the day. Calm down using three breaths when necessary. If you can't calm your emotions, be honest and use an I message to convey your feelings and model self-regulation strategies. For example, "I notice that I am beginning to feel very frustrated because I'm trying to give a lesson and people are talking so others can't hear me. I notice that when I get frustrated my shoulders get tense and I begin to feel hot. I notice that I need to calm down, so I'm going to take three long slow breaths right now." Demonstrate the breaths and even invite the class to join you. "I feel much better now. I am calm and you are all ready to listen, so I can finish my lesson." Postpone taking action until everyone calms down (Jennings, 2015a). Assume good intent and goodwill among students, families, and colleagues. When you notice it beginning to erode, find ways to recover using self-care strategies and mindful awareness and compassion practices (Jennings, 2019).

Chronic Behavior Problems

The best classroom management is proactive and preventative. However, there are often a few students who exhibit chronic behavior problems that don't respond to the typical approaches described above. When approaching chronic behavioral issues, begin by taking time to reflect on your interpretation of the behavior. Ask yourself, "What emotions are being triggered by the behavior? Am I taking the behavior personally? What biases from my past may affect my perceptions of the behavior? Practice taking three breaths to calm down, model self-regulation to communicate your feelings, and teach self-regulation when necessary. Take time to practice the loving-kindness practice at the end of Chapter 6 to help you cultivate feelings of compassion toward this student.

Routine Maintenance

Begin by checking the environment. Is there something in the classroom that is reinforcing or inducing this behavior? For example, maybe you've inadvertently created a runway in your classroom, which can be easily remedied by moving some furniture around. Maybe the classroom is overstimulating a highly sensitive student.

Check that the students' physical needs are met. Is she sick? Can he hear you? Is her blood sugar low? Is he dehydrated? Check to make sure that the expectation is developmentally appropriate for the student and check for understanding. Does the student know what the expectation is? Does he or she need reminding, reinforcing, redirecting? Finally, give a logical consequence with a calm, firm voice (you break it, you fix it; loss of privileges; positive time out).

Problem Solving

If issues continue, spend some time getting to know the student better. Invite him to spend some time with you one-on-one and ask some simple questions about things that are likely important to him such as pets, brothers or sisters, favorite activities, foods, and so on. Focus on one behavior at a time, considering which is most important to address first. Set up a time to speak to the student's parent to learn more about him, share your concerns, and perhaps develop a strategy using more home involvement (e.g., regular reports, check-ins, consequences at home). Be aware that chronic stress, trauma, and adversity may affect the student's behavior, and take time to become trauma informed and engage in trauma-sensitive practices. For more information on this issue, see my book *The Trauma-Sensitive Classroom* (Jennings, 2019).

Plan a problem-solving conference with the student. Begin by establishing the purpose of the conference, to address a specific behavior. For example, Mr. Parker set up a time to speak with Valentina about the trouble she was having getting along with her peers. She seemed to constantly engage in arguments with others that started with her grabbing learning materials away and hoarding them in her desk. Mr. Parker began by reaffirming the rapport that he had already established with her by asking about how things were going at home. "How's your new puppy?" he asked. Valentina beamed and said, "He's really fun! He's learning to fetch a ball!" "I have a dog too," he said. "His name is Buddy and he can fetch too."

Next Mr. Parker was careful to calmly describe the specific behavior and how it interferes with learning. "Valentina, when you take learning materials away from others when they are working, it interferes with learning. For example, today when you grabbed the glue away from Roberto, he couldn't finish the project he was working on. How do you think he felt?"

Mr. Parker continued to explore the situation with Valentina, asking her what she noticed and thought about what happened. Then he linked the behavior to the classroom expectations. "One of our classroom expectations is to respect one another. Was it respectful to grab the glue away from Roberto?" Finally he asked Valentina if she would be willing to work on the problem with him. Together they explored the cause of the problem, and he articulated clear, specific goals for them to work on. Finally, they generated solutions and chose one to try. "You know the three breaths activity that we've been learning to calm down? What if you used that practice when you begin to feel like grabbing something from one of your friends?" Finally he set up a regular check-in time to provide feedback and reinforcement (Crowe & Yang, 2009).

The next day, Mr. Parker watched Valentina with a mindful eye. When she was deeply engaged in a reading activity, he provided positive reinforcement by specifically naming the behavior and linking it to classroom expectations. "You are working so hard on the reading assignment. I can see that you are really doing your best!" When he noticed a moment when Valentina was watching Jennifer using a blue crayon that she obviously wanted, he stepped near her and reminded her of their conversation. "Valentina, it looks like you would like the blue crayon, but Jennifer is using it right now. Remember what we talked about yesterday? What can you do right now?" Valentina smiled and took three calming breaths. By the time she was done, she was ready to ask Jennifer if she could use the blue crayon. Immediately Mr. Parker provided positive reinforcement. "Valentina, you calmed yourself down and respectfully asked Jennifer for the blue crayon."

The problem-solving conference may not be enough to solve all classroom behavior challenges. In these cases, engage others to provide support. Discuss the problems with other teachers who know the student. Discuss issues with the principal or assistant principal, counselor, social worker, psychologist, and special education teachers. If necessary, create a behavior chart to support learning and reinforce improvement. Following school policies, engage other school personnel in problem solving (e.g., school counselor, special education teacher, social worker, administration). Parents should be informed and included according to school policies. These actions may lead to identification and referral to special education services.

Cultivating a Mindful Classroom

This book has provided a road map to cultivating a more mindful classroom. This includes developing your own mindfulness and applying it to your teaching, introducing developmentally appropriate mindful awareness practices to your students, and integrating these practices into various learning activities. Applying mindful awareness to the design and management of the classroom reinforces and sustains the benefits that result from integrating mindfulness into your curriculum. At the end of the book, there is an appendix full of resources that you can draw upon as you begin this journey of mindful teaching and learning.

References

Barrett, P., Zhang, Y., Davies, F., & Barrett, L. (2015). *Clever classrooms: Summary report of the HEAD Project*. Manchester, UK: University of Salford. Retrieved from https://www.salford.ac.uk/cleverclassrooms/1503-Salford-Uni-Report -DIGITAL.pdf

Blair, C., & Razza, R. P. (2007). Relating effortful control, executive function, and false belief understanding to emerging math and literacy ability in kindergarten. *Child Development, 78*, 647–663. https://doi.org/10.1111/j.1467-8624.2007 .01019.x

Brady, K., Forton, M. B., & Porter, D. (2003). *Rules in school: Teaching discipline in the responsive classroom*. Turners Falls, MA: Northeast Foundation for Children.

Brown, K. W., Kasser, T., Ryan, R. M., Alex Linley, P., & Orzech, K. (2009). When what one has is enough: Mindfulness, financial desire discrepancy, and subjective well-being. *Journal of Research in Personality, 43*, 727–736. http://dx.doi .org/10.1016/j.jrp.2009.07.002

Brown, K. W., & Ryan, R. M. (2003). The benefits of being present: Mindfulness and its role in psychological well-being. *Journal of Personality and Social Psychology, 84*, 822–848. http://doi.org/10.1037/0022-3514.84.4.822

CASEL. (n.d.). Retrieved June 25, 2018, from http://www.casel.org/

Chang, M.-L. (2009). An appraisal perspective of teacher burnout: Examining the emotional work of teachers. *Educational Psychology Review, 21*, 193–218. http://doi.org/10.1007/s10648-009-9106-y

Chartrand, T. L., & Lakin, J. L. (2013). The antecedents and consequences of human behavioral mimicry. *Annual Review of Psychology, 64*, 285–308. http://doi.org/10.1146/annurev-psych-113011-143754

Cohn, M. A., Fredrickson, B. L., Brown, S. L., Mikels, J. A., & Conway, A. M. (2009). Happiness unpacked: Positive emotions increase life satisfaction by building resilience. *Emotion, 9*, 361–368. http://doi.org/10.1037/a0015952

Collishaw, S. (2014). Annual research review: Secular trends in child and adolescent mental health. *Journal of Child Psychology and Psychiatry, 56*, 370–393. http://doi.org/10.1111/jcpp.12372

Crowe, C., & Yang, A. (2009). *Solving thorny behavior problems*. Turners Falls, MA: Northeast Foundation for Children.

Davidson, R. J., Dunne, J., Eccles, J. S., Engle, A., Greenberg, M., . . . Vago, D. (2012). Contemplative practices and mental training: Prospects for American education. *Child Development Perspectives, 6*, 146–153. http://doi.org/10.1111/j.1750-8606.2012.00240.x

Dekeyser, M., Raes, F., Leijssen, M., Leysen, S., & Dewulf, D. (2008). Mindfulness skills and interpersonal behaviour. *Personality and Individual Differences, 44*, 1235–1245. http://doi.org/10.1016/j.paid.2007.11.018

Denton, P., & Kriete, R. (2000). *The first six weeks of school*. Turners Falls, MA: Northeast Foundation for Children.

Diamond, A., & Lee, K. (2011). Interventions shown to aid executive function development in children 4 to 12 years old. *Science, 333*, 959–964. http://doi.org/10.1126/science.1204529

Dreikurs, R., Grunwald, B. B., & Pepper, F. C. (1998). *Maintaining sanity in the classroom: Classroom management techniques*. Philadelphia: Taylor and Francis.

Fadiga, L., Fogassi, G., Pavesi, G., & Rizzolatti, G. (1995). Motor facilitation during action observation: A magnetic stimulation study. *Journal of Neurophysiology, 73*, 2608–2611. https://doi-org.proxy01.its.virginia.edu/10.1152/jn.1995.73.6.2608

Fielding, R. (2006, March 1). What they see is what we get: A primer on light. Retrieved from https://www.edutopia.org/what-they-see-what-we-get

Gest, S. D., Madill, R. A., Zadzora, K. M., Miller, A. M., & Rodkin, P. C. (2014). Teacher management of elementary classroom social dynamics. *Journal of Emotional and Behavioral Disorders, 22,* 107–118. http://doi.org/10.1177/1063426613512677

Goetz, J. L., Keltner, D., & Simon-Thomas, E. (2010). Compassion: An evolutionary analysis and empirical review. *Psychological Bulletin, 136,* 351–374. http://doi.org/10.1037/a0018807

Hadhazy, A. (2010, February 12). Think twice: How the gut's "second brain" influences mood and well-being. *Scientific American.* Retrieved from https://www.scientificamerican.com/article/gut-second-brain/

Hobfoll, S. E. (2018). *Tribalism: The evolutionary origins of fear politics.* Cham, Switzerland: Palgrave Macmillan.

Jennings, P. A. (2015a). *Mindfulness for teachers: Simple skills for peace and productivity in the classroom.* New York: Norton.

Jennings, P. A. (2015b). Mindfulness-based programs and the American public school system: Recommendations for best practices to ensure secularity. *Mindfulness, 7,* 176–178. http://doi.org/10.1007/s12671-015-0477-5

Jennings, P. A. (2019). *The trauma-sensitive classroom: Building resilience with compassionate teaching.* New York: Norton.

Jennings, P. A., & Frank, J. L. (2015). Inservice preparation for educators. In J. A. Durlak, C. E. Domitrovich, R. P. Weissberg, & T. P. Gullotta (Eds.), *Handbook of social and emotional learning: Research and practice* (pp. 422–437). New York: Guilford.

Jennings, P. A., & Harris, A. R. (2018). *Thrive! The compassionate schools project curriculum.* Charlottesville: University of Virginia.

Kabat-Zinn, J. (2003). Mindfulness-based interventions in context: Past, present and future. *Clinical Psychology: Science and Practice, 10,* 144-156.

Kabat-Zinn, J. (2009). *Full catastrophe living: Using the wisdom of your body and mind to face stress, pain, and illness.* New York, NY: Delta.

Kenney, E. L., Long, M. W., Cradock, A. L., & Gortmaker, S. L. (2015). Prevalence of inadequate hydration among US children and disparities by gender and race/ethnicity: National health and nutrition examination survey, 2009–2012. *American Journal of Public Health, 105,* 113–118. http://doi.org/10.2105/AJPH.2015.302572

Khng, K. H. (2017). A better state-of-mind: Deep breathing reduces state anxiety and enhances test performance through regulating test cognitions in children. *Cognition and Emotion, 31,* 1502–1510. http://doi.org/10.1080/02699931.2016.1233095

Khoury, B., Sharma, M., Rush, S. E., & Fournier, C. (2015). Mindfulness-based stress reduction for healthy individuals: A meta-analysis. *Journal of Psychosomatic Research, 78,* 519–528. http://doi.org/10.1016/j.jpsychores.2015.03.009

Kounin, J. S. (1970). *Discipline and group management in classrooms.* Oxford: Holt, Rinehart and Winston.

Ladson-Billings, G. (1995). But that's just good teaching! The case for culturally relevant pedagogy. *Theory Into Practice, 34*(3), 159–165.

Lawlor, M. S. (2016). Mindfulness and social emotional learning (SEL): A conceptual framework. In K. A. Schonert-Reichl & R. W. Roeser (Eds.), *Handbook of mindfulness in education integrating theory and research into practice* (pp. 65–82). New York: Springer-Verlag.

Lillard, A. S. (2005). *Montessori: The science behind the genius.* New York: Oxford University Press.

McEwen, B. S., & Wingfield, J. C. (2003). The concept of allostasis in biology and biomedicine. *Hormones and Behavior, 43,* 2–15. http://doi.org/10.1016/S0018-506X(02)00024-7

Moffitt, T. E., Arseneault, L., Belsky, D., Dickson, N., Hancox, R. J., Harrington, H., . . . Caspi, A. (2011). A gradient of childhood self-control predicts health, wealth, and public safety. *Proceedings of the National Academy of Sciences, 108,* 2693–2698. http://doi.org/10.1073/pnas.1010076108

Murray, J., Scott, H., Connolly, C., & Wells, A. (2018). The attention training technique improves children's ability to delay gratification: A controlled comparison with progressive relaxation. *Behaviour Research and Therapy, 104,* 1–6. http://doi.org/10.1016/j.brat.2018.02.003

Payne, V., & Isaacs, L. (2016). *Human motor development: A lifespan approach.* New York: Routledge.

Pearce, J. C. (1977). *Magical child.* New York: E. P. Dutton.

Perciavalle, V., Blandini, M., Fecarotta, P., Buscemi, A., Di Corrado, D., Bertolo,

L., . . . Coco, M. (2016). The role of deep breathing on stress. *Neurological Sciences, 38,* 451–458. http://doi.org/10.1007/s10072-016-2790-8

Remen, R. N. (2006). *Kitchen table wisdom: Stories that heal.* New York: Riverhead.

Ricard, M. (2015). *Altruism: The power of compassion to change yourself and the world* (C. Mandell & S. Gordon, Trans.). New York: Little, Brown.

Ryan, T. (2014, April 24). Congressman Tim Ryan speaks at the Contemplative Science Center at U.Va. Retrieved from http://www.uvacontemplation.org/content/congressman-tim-ryan-speaks-contemplative-science-center-uva

Satter, E. (2008). *Secrets of feeding a healthy family* (2nd ed.). Madison, WI: Kelcy Press.

Siegel, D. J. (2009). *Mindsight: The new science of personal transformation.* New York: Bantam.

Teper, R., Segal, Z. V., & Inzlicht, M. (2013). Inside the mindful mind. *Current Directions in Psychological Science, 22,* 449–454. http://doi.org/10.1177/0963721413495869

Turkovich, M. (n.d.). The Charter for Compassion. Retrieved from https://charterforcompassion.org/charter/charter-overvew

Vago, D. R., & David, S. A. M. D. (2012). Self-awareness, self-regulation, and self-transcendence (S-ART): A framework for understanding the neurobiological mechanisms of mindfulness. *Frontiers in Human Neuroscience, 6,* 296. http://doi.org/10.3389/fnhum.2012.00296/abstract

Warneken, F., & Tomasello, M. (2007). Helping and cooperation at 14 months of age. *Infancy, 11,* 271–294. doi:10.1080/15250000701310389

Williams, J. M. G., & Kabat-Zinn, J. (2011). Mindfulness: Diverse perspectives on its meaning, origins, and multiple applications at the intersection of science and dharma. *Contemporary Buddhism, 12*(1), 1–18. doi:10.1080/14639947.2011.564811.

Witt, M. (2011). School based working memory training: Preliminary finding of improvement in children's mathematical performance. *Advances in Cognitive Psychology, 7,* 7–15. http://doi.org/10.2478/v10053-008-0083-3

Wood, A. (2015). *The napping house.* New York: HMH Books for Young Readers.

Xie, L., Kang, H., Xu, Q., Chen, M. J., Liao, Y., Thiyagarajan, M., . . . Nedergaard, M. (2013). Sleep drives metabolite clearance from the adult brain. *Science, 342,* 373–377. http://doi.org/10.1126/science.1241224

Yantis, S. (1996). Attentional capture in vision. In A. F. Kramer, M. G. H. Coles., & G. D. Logan (Eds.), *Converging operations in the study of visual selective attention* (pp. 45–67). Washington, DC: American Psychological Association.

Zelazo, P. D., & Lyons, K. E. (2012). The potential benefits of mindfulness training in early childhood: A developmental social cognitive neuroscience perspective. *Child Development Perspectives, 6,* 154–160. http://doi.org/10.1111/j.1750-8606.2012.00241.x

Resources

This section will help you find resources to support your developing mindfulness practice and teach mindful awareness practices to your students. The section begins with a bibliography with book suggestions for general mindfulness, mindfulness in education, and children's books. The next section lists URLs for mindfulness-based programs for children, youth and teachers. An overall resource to access all things mindful is Mindful Magazine (www.mindful.org) which is published on line and in print. The website has a resources section with links to a vast array of mindfulness resources: http://www.mindful.org/resources

Further Reading

BIBLIOGRAPHY OF GENERAL MINDFULNESS BOOKS

Anh-Huong, N., & Hanh, T.N. (2006). Walking meditation. Boulder, CO: Sounds True, Inc.

Baraz, J., & Alexander, S. (2010). Awakening joy: 10 steps that will put you on the road to real happiness. New York, NY: Bantam Books.

Bauer-Wu, S. (2011). Leaves falling gently: Living fully with serious and life-limiting illness through mindfulness, compassion, and connectedness. Oakland, CA: New Harbinger Publications.

Begley, S. (2007). Train your mind, change your brain: How a new science reveals our extraordinary potential to transform ourselves. New York, NY: Ballantine Books.

Bloom, P. (Ed.). (2010). The power of compassion: Stories that open the heart, heal the soul, and change the world. Charlottesville, VA: Hampton Roads Publishing.

Boorstein, S. (1997). It's easier than you think: The Buddhist way to happiness. New York, NY: HarperCollins.

Boorstein, S. (2008). Happiness is an inside job: Practicing for a joyful life. New York, NY: Ballantine Books.

Boyce, B., & the editors of Shambhala Sun (Eds.). (2011). The mindfulness revolution: Leading psychologists, scientists, artists, and meditation teachers on the power of mindfulness in daily life. Boston, MA: Shambhala Publications.

Brach, T. (2004). Radical acceptance: Embracing your life with the heart of a Buddha. New York, NY: Bantam Books.

Brach, T. (2013). True refuge: Finding peace and freedom in your own awakened heart. New York, NY: Bantam Books.

Bush, M. (Ed.). (2011). Contemplation nation: How ancient practices are changing how we live. North Charleston, SC: CreateSpace Independent Publishing Platform.

Chödrön, P. (2000). When things fall apart: Heart advice for difficult times. Boston, MA: Shambhala Publications.

Chödrön, P. (2002). The places that scare you: A guide to fearlessness in difficult times. Boston, MA: Shambhala Publications.

Chödrön, P. (2003). Comfortable with uncertainty: 108 teachings on cultivating fearlessness and compassion. Boston, MA: Shambhala Publications.

Chödrön, P. (2004). Start where you are: A guide to compassionate living. Boston, MA: Shambhala Publications.

Chödrön, P. (2010). Taking the leap: Freeing ourselves from old habits and fears. Boston, MA: Shambhala Publications.

Coleman, M. (2016). Make peace with your mind: How mindfulness and compassion can free you from your inner critic. Novato, CA: New World Library.

Colier, N. (2016). The power of off: The mindful way to stay sane in a virtual world. Louisville, CO: Sounds True.

Csikszentmihalyi, M. (2008). Flow: The psychology of optimal experience. New York, NY: Harper Perennial Modern Classics.

Doidge, N. (2007). The brain that changes itself: Stories of personal triumph from the frontiers of brain science. New York, NY: Penguin.

Goldstein, J. (2003). Insight meditation: The practice of freedom. Boston, MA: Shambhala Publications.

Goldstein, J. (2013). Mindfulness: A practical guide to awakening. Boulder, CO: Sounds True, Inc.

Goldstein, J., & Kornfield, J. (2001). Seeking the heart of wisdom: The path of insight meditation. Boston, MA: Shambhala Publications.

Goleman, D. (1996). The meditative mind: The varieties of meditative experience. New York, NY: Tarcher.

Goleman, D., & Davidson, R. J. (2017). *Altered traits: science reveals how meditation changes your mind, brain, and body.* New York, NY: Penguin.

Gunaratana, B. (2011). Mindfulness in plain English. Somerville, MA: Wisdom Publications.

Hanh, T.N. (1992). Peace is every step: The path of mindfulness in everyday life. New York, NY: Bantam Books.

Hanh, T.N. (1999). The miracle of mindfulness: An introduction to the practice of meditation (M. Ho, Trans.). Boston, MA: Beacon Press.

Hanh, T.N. (2008). Breathe, you are alive: The sutra on the full awareness of breathing. Berkeley, CA: Parallax Press.

Hanh, T.N. (2010). You are here: Discovering the magic of the present moment. Boston, MA: Shambhala Publications.

Hanson, R. (2013). Hardwiring happiness: The new brain science of contentment, calm, and confidence. New York, NY: Harmony.

Hanson, R., & Mendius, R. (2009). Buddha's brain: The practical neuroscience of happiness, love, and wisdom. Oakland, CA: New Harbinger Publications.

Harris, D. (2014). 10% happier: How i tamed the voice in my head, reduced stress without losing my edge, and found self-help that actually works-a true story. New York, NY: Harper Collins.

Hart, T. (2014). The four virtues: Presence, heart, wisdom, creation. New York, NY: Atria Books/Beyond Words.

Hart, T., Nelson, P.L., & Puhakka, K. (Eds.). (2000). Transpersonal knowing: Exploring the horizon of consciousness. Albany, NY: State University of New York Press.

Kabat-Zinn, J. (2005). Wherever you go, there you are: Mindfulness meditation in everyday life. New York, NY: Hyperion.

Kabat-Zinn, J. (2006). Coming to our senses: Healing ourselves and the world through mindfulness. New York, NY: Hyperion.

Kabat-Zinn, J. (2007). Arriving at your own door: 108 lessons in mindfulness. New York, NY: Hyperion.

Kabat-Zinn, J. (2009). Full catastrophe living: Using the wisdom of your body and mind to face stress, pain, and illness. New York, NY: Delta Trade.

Kabat-Zinn, J. (2009). Letting everything become your teacher: 100 lessons in mindfulness. New York, NY: Delta Trade.

Kabat-Zinn, J. (2011). Mindfulness for beginners: Reclaiming the present moment--and your life. Boulder, CO: Sounds True, Inc.

Kornfield, J. (1993). A path with heart: A guide through the perils and promises of spiritual life. New York, NY: Bantam.

Kornfield, J. (2001). After the ecstasy, the laundry: How the heart grows wise on the spiritual path. New York, NY: Bantam Books.

Kornfield, J. (2008). The art of forgiveness, lovingkindness, and peace. New York, NY: Bantam Books.

Kornfield, J. (2009). The wise heart: A guide to the universal teachings of Buddhist psychology. New York, NY: Bantam Books.

Langer, E.J. (1990). Mindfulness. Boston, MA: Da Capo Press.

Langer, E.J. (2009). Counterclockwise: Mindful health and the power of possibility. New York, NY: Ballantine Books.

Levine, S. (1991). Guided meditations, explorations and healings. New York, NY: Anchor Books.

Levine, S. (1998). A year to live: How to live this year as if it were your last. New York, NY: Bell Tower.

Merton, T. (2007). New seeds of contemplation. New York, NY: New Directions.

O'Hara, P.E. (2014). Most intimate: A Zen approach to life's challenges. Boston, MA: Shambhala Publications.

Ryan, T. (2013). A mindful nation: How a simple practice can help us reduce stress, improve performance, and recapture the American spirit. Carlsbad, CA: Hay House.

Salgado, B. (2016). Real world mindfulness for beginners: Navigate daily life one practice at a time. Berkeley, CA: Sonoma Press.

Salzberg, S. (1999). A heart as wide as the world: Stories on the path to lovingkindness. Boston, MA: Shambhala Publications.

Salzberg, S. (2004). Lovingkindness: The revolutionary art of happiness. Boston, MA: Shambhala Publications.

Salzberg, S. (2010). Real happiness: The power of meditation: A 28-day program. New York, NY: Workman Publishing Company.

Salzberg, S. (2017). Real love: The art of mindful connection. New York, NY: Flatiron.

Santorelli, S. (2000). Heal thy self: Lessons on mindfulness in medicine. New York, NY: Harmony/Bell Tower.

Senge, P., Scharmer, C.O., Jaworski, J., & Flowers, B.S. (2005). Presence: An exploration of profound change in people, organizations, and society. New York, NY: Currency.

Siegel, D.J. (2007). The mindful brain: Reflection and attunement in the cultivation of well-being. New York, NY: W.W. Norton & Company.

Siegel, D.J. (2014). Brainstorm: The power and purpose of the teenage brain. New York, NY: Tarcher.

Smalley, S.L., & Winston, D. (2010). Fully present: The science, art, and practice of mindfulness. Philadelphia, PA: Da Capo Lifelong Books.

Stahl, B., & Goldstein, E. (2010). A Mindfulness-Based Stress Reduction workbook. Oakland, CA: New Harbinger Publications.

Teasdale, J., Williams, M., & Segal, Z. (2014). The mindful way workbook: An 8-week program to free yourself from depression and emotional distress. New York, NY: The Guilford Press.

Tolle, E. (2003). Stillness speaks. Novato, CA: New World Library.

Tolle, E. (2004). The power of now: A guide to spiritual enlightenment. Novato, CA: New World Library.

Tolle, E. (2008). A new earth: Awakening to your life's purpose. New York, NY: Penguin.

Wallace, A. (2006). The attention revolution: Unlocking the power of the focused mind. Somerville, MA: Wisdom Publications.

Williams, M., & Penman, D. (2012). Mindfulness: An eight-week plan for finding peace in a frantic world. New York, NY: Rodale Books.

Zajonc, A. (2008). Meditation as contemplative inquiry. Great Barrington, MA: Lindisfarne Books.

BIBLIOGRAPHY OF MINDFULNESS IN EDUCATION BOOKS

Bersma, D., & Visscher, M. (2003). Yoga games for children: Fun and fitness with postures, movements and breath. Alameda, CA: Hunter House.

Broderick, P.C. (2013). Learning to Breathe: A mindfulness curriculum for adolescents to cultivate emotion regulation, attention, and performance. Oakland, CA: New Harbinger Publications.

Broderick, P.C. (2019). Mindfulness in the secondary classroom: A guide for teaching adolescents (SEL Solutions Series). New York, NY: W.W. Norton.

Chanchani, S., & Chanchani, R. (2007). Yoga for children: A complete illustrated guide to yoga. New Dehli, India: UBS Publishers' Distributors.

Cohen Harper, J. (2013). Little flower yoga for kids: A yoga and mindfulness program to help your child improve attention and emotional balance. Oakland, CA: New Harbinger Publications.

Flynn, L. (2013). Yoga for children: 200+ yoga poses, breathing exercises, and meditations for healthier, happier, more resilient children. Avon, MA: Adams Media.

Hanh, T.N., & the Plum Village Community. (2011). Planting seeds: Practicing mindfulness with children. Berkeley, CA: Parallax Press.

Hart, T. (2003). The secret spiritual world of children: The breakthrough discovery that profoundly alters our conventional view of children's mystical experiences. Novato, CA: New World Library.

Hart, T. (2009). From information to transformation: Education for the evolution of consciousness (Rev. ed.). New York, NY: Peter Lang International Academic Publishers.

Hoobyar, H. (2013). Yoga for kids: The basics. North Charleston, SC: CreateSpace Independent Publishing Platform.

Johnson, A.N., & Webb Neagley, M. (Eds.). (2011). Educating from the heart: Theoretical and practical approaches to transforming education. Lanham, MD: Rowman & Littlefield Education.

Jennings, P. A. (2015). Mindfulness for teachers: Simple skills for peace and productivity in the classroom. New York, NY: W. W. Norton.

Jennings, P. A. (2019). The trauma-sensitive classroom: Building resilience with compassionate teaching. New York, NY: W. W. Norton.

Jennings, P. A. (Ed.), DeMauro, A. A., & Mischenko, P. (Assoc. Eds.) (2019). *The mindful school: Transforming school culture with mindfulness and compassion.* New York, NY: Guilford.

Kaiser Greenland, S. (2010). The mindful child: How to help your kid manage stress and become happier, kinder, and more compassionate. New York, NY: Free Press.

Kessler, R. (2000). The soul of education: Helping students find connection, compassion, and character at school. Alexandria, VA: Association for Supervision and Curriculum Development.

Krishnamurti, J. (2008). Education and the significance of life. New York, NY: HarperOne.

Langer, E.J. (1998). The power of mindful learning. Boston, MA: Da Capo Press.

Lantieri, L. (2008). Building emotional intelligence: Techniques to cultivate inner strength in children. Boulder, CO: Sounds True, Inc.

Lichtmann, M. (2005). The teacher's way: Teaching and the contemplative life. Mahwah, NJ: Paulist Press.

MacDonald, E., & Shirley, D. (2009). The mindful teacher. New York, NY: Teachers College Press.

McHenry, I., & Brady, R. (Eds.). (2009). Tuning in: Mindfulness in teaching and learning. Philadelphia, PA: Friends Council in Education.

Miller, J. (1994). The contemplative practitioner: Meditation in education and the professions. Westport, CT: Bergin & Garvey.

Murray, L.E. (2012). Calm kids: Help children relax with mindful activities. Edinburgh, UK: Floris Books.

O'Reilley, M.R. (1998). Radical presence: Teaching as contemplative practice. Portsmouth, NH: Boynton/Cook Publishers.

Palmer, P. (2007). The courage to teach: Exploring the inner landscape of a teacher's life. San Francisco, CA: Jossey-Bass.

Rawlinson, A. (2013). Creative yoga for children: Inspiring the whole child through yoga, songs, literature, and games. Berkeley, CA: North Atlantic Books.

Rechtschaffen, D. (2014). The way of mindful education: Cultivating well-being in teachers and students. New York, NY: W. W. Norton & Company.

Reddy, R. (2014). The art of mindfulness for children: Mindfulness exercises that will raise happier, confident, compassionate, and calmer children. North Charleston, SC: CreateSpace Independent Publishing Platform.

Saltzman, A. (2014). A still quiet place: A mindfulness program for teaching children and adolescents to ease stress and difficult emotions. Oakland, CA: New Harbinger Publications.

Saltzman, A., & Willard, C. (Eds.). (2014). Mindfulness with youth: From the classroom to the clinic. New York, NY: Guilford Press.

Schoeberlein, D., & Sheth, S. (2009). Mindful teaching and teaching mindfulness: A guide for anyone who teaches anything. Somerville, MA: Wisdom Publications.

Srinivasan, M. (2014). Teach, breathe, learn: Mindfulness in and out of the classroom. Berkeley, CA: Parallax Press.

Vallely, S.W. (2008). Sensational meditation for children: Child-friendly meditation techniques based on the five senses. Asheville, NC: Satya International.

Weaver, L., & Wilding, M. (2013). The 5 dimensions of engaged teaching: A practical guide for educators. Bloomington, IN: Solution Tree Press.

Wenig, M. (2003). YogaKids: Educating the whole child through yoga. New York, NY: Stewart, Tabori and Chang.

Willard, C. (2010). Child's mind: Mindfulness practices to help our children be more focused, calm, and relaxed. Berkeley, CA: Parallax Press.

BIBLIOGRAPHY OF MINDFUL PARENTING BOOKS

Bardacke, N. (2012). Mindful birthing: Training the mind, body, and heart for childbirth and beyond. New York, NY: HarperOne.

Hawn, G., & Holden, W. (2012). 10 mindful minutes: Giving our children--and ourselves--the social and emotional skills to reduce stress and anxiety for healthier, happy lives. New York, NY: Perigee Trade.

Kabat-Zinn, M., & Kabat-Zinn, J. (1998). Everyday blessings: The inner work of mindful parenting. New York, NY: Hyperion.

Miller, K.M. (2007). Momma Zen: Walking the crooked path of motherhood. Boston, MA: Trumpeter Books.

Race, K. (2014). Mindful parenting: Simple and powerful solutions for raising creative, engaged, happy kids in today's hectic world. New York, NY: St. Martin's Griffin.

Roy, D. (2007). Momfulness: Mothering with mindfulness, compassion, and grace. San Francisco, CA: Jossey-Bass.

Ruethling, A., & Pitcher, P. (2003). Under the Chinaberry tree: Books and inspirations for mindful parenting. New York, NY: Broadway Books.

Shapiro, S., & White, C. (2014). Mindful discipline: A loving approach to setting limits and raising an emotionally intelligent child. Oakland, CA: New Harbinger Publications.

Siegel, D.J., & Bryson, T.P. (2012). The whole-brain child: 12 revolutionary strategies to nurture your child's developing mind. New York, NY: Bantam Books.

Siegel, D.J., & Hartzell, M. (2004). Parenting from the inside out. New York, NY: Tarcher.

Vieten, C., & Boorstein, S. (2009). Mindful motherhood: Practical tools for staying sane during pregnancy and your child's first year. Oakland, CA: New Harbinger Publications.

BIBLIOGRAPHY OF CHILDREN'S BOOKS

Alderfer, L. (2011). Mindful monkey, happy panda. Somerville, MA: Wisdom Publications.

Biegel, G.M. (2010). The stress reduction workbook for teens: Mindfulness skills to help you deal with stress. Oakland, CA: Instant Help Books.

Clarke, C. (2012). Imaginations: Fun relaxation stories and meditations for kids. North Charleston, SC: CreateSpace Independent Publishing Platform.

Davies, A. (2010). My first yoga: Animal poses. Cambridge, MA: My First Yoga.

DiOrio, R. (2010). What does it mean to be present? Belvedere, CA: Little Pickle Press.

Eddy, L. (2010). Every body does yoga. Houston, TX: Strategic Book Publishing.

Hanh, T.N. (2002). Under the rose apple tree. Berkeley, CA: Plum Blossom Books.

Hanh, T.N. (2008). Mindful movements: Ten exercises for well-being. Berkeley, CA: Parallax Press.

Hanh, T.N. (2010). A pebble for your pocket. Berkeley, CA: Plum Blossom Books.

Hanh, T.N. (2012). A handful of quiet: Happiness in four pebbles. Berkeley, CA: Plum Blossom Books.

Lite, L. (2008). Angry octopus: A relaxation story. Marietta, GA: Stress Free Kids.

MacLean, K.L. (2004). Peaceful piggy meditation. Park Ridge, IL: Albert Whitman & Company.

MacLean, K.L. (2009). Moody cow meditates. Somerville, MA: Wisdom Publications.

MacLean, K.L. (2014). Peaceful piggy yoga. Park Ridge, IL: Albert Whitman & Company.

McGinnis, M.W. (2013). An orange for you: A child's book of awareness. North Charleston, SC: CreateSpace Independent Publishing Platform.

Muth, J.J. (2005). Zen shorts. New York, NY: Scholastic Press.

Muth, J.J. (2008). Zen ties. New York, NY: Scholastic Press.

Silver, G. (2009). Anh's anger. Berkeley, CA: Plum Blossom Books.

Snel, E. (2013). Sitting still like a frog: Mindfulness exercises for kids (and their parents). Boston, MA: Shambhala Publications.

Thomson, B., & Hoffsteader, N. (2013). Meditation, my friend: Meditation for kids and beginners of all ages. New York, NY: Betsy Thomson.

Verdick, E. (2010). Calm-down time. Minneapolis, MN: Free Spirit Publishing.

Yoo, T.E. (2012). You are a lion! And other fun yoga poses. New York, NY: Nancy Paulsen Books.

Mindfulness-Based Programs for Students and Teachers

This resource section contains links to school-based, mindfulness-based programs for teachers and students.

Calm Classroom
Chicago, IL
http://calmclassroom.com

Calmer Choice
Cotuit, MA
http://calmerchoice.org

Center for Courage and Renewal
Courage to Teach
Seattle, WA and other locations worldwide
http://www.couragerenewal.org/courage-to-teach

CREATE for Education
Offers CARE and CALM programs for teachers
https://createforeducation.org/

Cultivating Awareness and Resilience in Education (CARE for Teachers)
CREATE for Education
https://createforeducation.org/

Education for Excellence
New York, NY and other locations worldwide
http://educationforexcellence.com

Every Kids Yoga
New York, NY
http://www.everykidsyoga.com

Flourish Foundation
Ketchum, ID
http://flourishfoundation.org

Friends Council on Education
Philadelphia, PA and other US locations
http://www.friendscouncil.org

Growing Minds
Milwaukee, WI
http://www.growingmindstoday.com

Holistic Life Foundation
Baltimore, MD and other US locations
http://hlfinc.org

Inner Explorer
Franklin, MA
http://innerexplorer.org

Inner Kids
Los Angeles, CA and other US locations
https://www.susankaisergreenland.com/inner-kids-model/

Inward Bound Mindfulness Education
North Andover, MA and other US locations
http://ibme.info

Kripalu
Stockbridge, MA and other US locations
https://kripalu.org/educators

Learning to BREATHE
Philadelphia, PA and other US locations
http://learning2breathe.org

Little Flower Yoga
Croton on Hudson, NY and other US locations
http://littlefloweryoga.com

Mind Body Awareness Project
Oakland, CA
http://www.mbaproject.org

Mindfulness-Based Emotional Balance
http://www.margaretcullen.com/programs/

Mindfulness in Schools (.b)
Oxford, UK and other locations worldwide
http://mindfulnessinschools.org

Mindfulness Without Borders
Tiburon, CA and other locations worldwide
http://mindfulnesswithoutborders.org

Mindful Schools
Oakland, CA and other US locations
http://www.mindfulschools.org/

MindUp
Locations worldwide
http://teacher.scholastic.com/products/mindup/

Naropa University
Contemplative Education Program
Boulder, CO
https://www.naropa.edu/the-naropa-experience/contemplative-education/index.php

PassageWorks Institute
Boulder, CO
Offers SMART program for teachers
http://passageworks.org/

Relax to Learn
Baton Rouge, LA
http://relaxtolearn.com

Shanti Generation
http://shantigeneration.com/
Still Quiet Place
Menlo Park, CA and other US locations
http://www.stillquietplace.com

SMART in Education (Two organizations deliver this program)

    1. Passageworks
    Boulder, CO and other US locations
    http://passageworks.org
    http://passageworks.org/courses/smart-in-education/

    2. University of British Columbia, Okanagan Campus
    Kelowna, BC Canada and other locations in Canada
    http://ok-edu.sites.olt.ubc.ca

Thrive! The Compassionate Schools Project Curriculum
University of Virginia, Charlottesville VA and other US locations
https://www.compassionschools.org/

Transformative Life Skills
Oakland, CA and other locations worldwide
http://www.niroga.org/

Wake Up Schools
Escondido, CA
http://wakeupschools.org

Wellness Works in Schools
Lancaster, PA
http://www.wellnessworksinschools.com

Yoga in Schools
Pittsburgh, PA and other US locations
http://yogainschools.org

Other Resources

Best Meditation Apps of 2018
https://www.healthline.com/health/mental-health/top-meditation-iphone-android-apps

Center for Mindfulness
Offers Mindfulness-Based Stress Reduction worldwide
https://www.umassmed.edu/cfm/

Mindfulness Meditation: Guided Practices
https://www.mindful.org/mindfulness-meditation-guided-practices/

Top 20 Mindfulness Apps For Meditation, Eating & Awareness
https://positivepsychologyprogram.com/mindfulness-apps/

What Mindfulness App Is Right for You?
https://www.huffpost.com/entry/what-mindfulness-app-is-right-for-you_b_8026010

Songs that Promote Prosocial Behavior
Edutopia
https://www.edutopia.org/music-develop-social-emotional-character

How to Make Mind or Glitter Jars

https://www.mindful.org/how-to-create-a-glitter-jar-for-kids/

https://www.goodtoknow.co.uk/family/things-to-do/glitter-jars-how-to-calm-down
-jar-105300

https://preschoolinspirations.com/6-ways-to-make-a-calm-down-jar/

https://heartmindkids.com/how-to-make-a-glitter-jar-for-mindfulness/

https://blissfulkids.com/mindfulness-kids-teens-calming-glitter-jar-aka-mind-jar/

Eco-Friendly Alternatives

https://www.buzzfeed.com/johngara/simple-pretty-mindfulness-jars-diy

How to Make an Energyometer

To make an Energyometer, draw an oblong thermometer shape on a piece of cardboard or poster board. You can make a large one for demonstration purposes or students can make smaller ones for individual use. On the side you can create a scale with numbers from 1-10, or you can just put ticks on the side and write the words "low," "medium" and "high" at the bottom, middle and top along the side of the thermometer. Cut a hole in the bottom and the top of the place where the mercury would be located in the thermometer. Thread a bead on a piece of yarn long enough to thread through the two holes. Tape the thread on the back of the energyometer to hold it in place. To indicate your energy level move the bead up or down along the yarn.

How to Make a Pinwheel

Create a template by folding an 8 ½" by 11" piece of paper on the diagonal to create a square. Draw a line to indicate the extra part of the paper that will need to be cut off to make the square. Draw a 2" diameter circle in the center of the square and dotted lines from each corner of the square to the circle. You can photocopy this template so each student will have a copy.

Invite the students to cut out the square and color it on both sides. Then invite them to cut along the diagonal, dotted lines to the circle. Use a pushpin to poke holes in the center of the pinwheel and in each of the four corners. Turn the pin several times to make the holes larger to help the pinwheel spin smoothly. Stick the pushpin through each of the corner holes, through the center hole, then into a pencil eraser. Invite the students to blow the pinwheel with long slow mindful breaths.

How to Make Breathing Buddies

Rock Breathing Buddies. Invite the students to bring in a smooth rock about the size of their palm. If this is a challenge, you can purchase such rocks at your local craft store. Or, better yet, you can go on a field trip to a stream or riverbed to hunt for appropriate rocks. Once everyone has a rock, invite the students to think about the rock as their buddy that will help them practice belly breathing. Invite them to draw or paint a face on the rock with markers or paint. Then practice deep belly breathing by putting the buddy on their belly so they can feel some resistance against it.

Bean Bag Breathing Buddies. Even young children can make bean bags out of felt. Depending upon the age of your students, you can prepare pieces of felt for them to sew. For younger students, sew together two square pieces of felt leaving one side open. For older students, let them do this themselves. Invite your students to create faces by gluing pieces of felt to their bean bag. Once they are dry, they can fill them with beans and then sew up the open side.

Index

Note: Italicized page locators refer to illustrations.

About the Author

PATRICIA A. JENNINGS is an Associate Professor of Education in the Curry School of Education at the University of Virginia. A regular mindfulness practitioner for over 45 years, she has spent most of her life exploring how mindfulness can enhance teaching and learning. After 22 years as a classroom teacher, school director, and teacher educator, Dr. Jennings received her doctorate in human development from the University of California, Davis and studied health psychology at the University of California, San Francisco. Now an internationally recognized leader in the fields of social and emotional learning and mindfulness in education, her current research focuses on mindfulness- and compassion-based approaches to improving the social and emotional classroom context and student learning. Dr. Jennings was awarded the Cathy Kerr Award for Courageous and Compassionate Science by the Mind & Life Institute in 2018 and was also recognized by Mindful Magazine as one of "Ten Mindfulness Researchers You Should Know." She is the author of *Mindfulness for Teachers: Simple Skills for Peace and Productivity in the Classroom* and *The Trauma-Sensitive Classroom: Building Resilience with Compassionate Teaching*.